Special Educational Needs and the Education Reform Act

Special Educational Needs and the Education Reform Act

edited by
Neville Jones and Jim Docking

tb

Trentham Books

First published in 1992 by Trentham Books Ltd

Trentham Books Limited
Westview House
734 London Road
Oakhill
Stoke-on-Trent
England ST4 5NP

British Library Cataloguing in Publication Data
A catalogue record for this book is available from the British
Library.

ISBN: 0 948080 54 X

Designed and typeset by Trentham Print Design Ltd, Chester
and printed in Great Britain by BPCC Wheatons Ltd, Exeter.

To Eileen and Anne

Contents

view of teaching history to children with special needs through the National Curriculum, and they explain in detail the reasons for their optimism.

As with history, the Secretary of State has made inroads on the National Curriculum in relation to geography. In recognition of the fact that this subject covers issues just as value-laden and politically controversial, the Secretary significantly altered the recommendations of the National Curriculum Council on those matters relating to environmental conflict and political decision-making. The emphasis now is to be on 'knowledge and understanding' rather than 'people's attitudes and opinions'. Issues like poor housing, traffic congestion and unemployment will not be agenda items for pupils learning geography, although these are possibly just as relevant to the day-to-day and post-school experiences of pupils as learning about the regions of the European Economic Community. If there is to be no provision in history or geography for discussing controversial contemporary matters of human interest and social conflict, then this sets limits to the contribution which these subjects can make to cross-curricular studies on citizenship.

Nigel Proctor cogently argues the case for geography as part of the National Curriculum, recognising its interdisciplinary nature through its links with science, the humanities and mathematics. With reference to the work of H. Gardner, he examines the theory of multiple intelligences as a way forward in teaching pupils with special needs. He then considers five aspects of communication — literacy, oracy, numeracy, graphicacy and physiognomy — and their translation into five forms of language. Detailed accounts are given of how all this has relevance for pupils with special needs. Lastly, Proctor reviews the National Curriculum arrangements for geography and criticises the revisions to the working party recommendations in the Statutory Orders, pointing out the ways in which these ignore the interests of all pupils, but especially those with special needs.

In their chapter on careers education and guidance, Mary Greaves and Dorothy Syndenham draw on their extensive experience of working in local education authority career services, providing a detailed account of how provision meets the needs of all pupils, but particularly those with special needs. They emphasise the need for teamwork, especially when working with the disabled. They refer extensively to the literature, guidelines, employment opportunities, and special schemes for the disabled. As with other contributors to this book, they raise a concern about the effect that LMS might have on support for pupils with special needs and the integration of the disabled into ordinary provision.

The last chapter of this book focuses on problems of assessment and recording achievement. Assessment in the National Curriculum, as promulgated by the Task Group on Assessment and Testing (TGAT), should serve several purposes. It should be: *formative*, 'so that the positive achievements of a pupil may be recognised and discussed and the appropriate next steps may be planned': *diagnostic*, 'through which learning difficulties may be scrutinised and classified so that appropriate remedial help and guidance can be provided'; *summative,* 'for the recording of the overall achievement of a pupil in a systematic way; and *evaluative,* 'by means of which some aspects of the work of a school, an LEA or other discrete part of the educational service can be assessed and/or reported upon'. These objectives, which have been taken on board by the Schools Examinations and Assessment Council, are to be achieved in two ways: through teachers' assessment and the use of standardised assessment tasks (SATs). Further, the Government has agreed that the published results for each school should take the form of aggregated raw data, unadjusted for intake or social background factors.

As many critics have pointed out, assessing the quality of a school, especially with regard to children with special learning needs, will need to include much more than pupils' absolute levels of achievement in the National Curriculum. This is because the *amount of progress* pupils make is a better indicator of the quality of educational provision. Desmond Nuttall and Harvey Goldstein (*Times Educational Supplement,* 15.2.91) have demonstrated from their analysis of the 1988 GCSE results in London that the public will be grossly misled in their judgements of a school's effectiveness unless factors such as the pupils' prior achievements and socio-economic conditions are taken into account. The evidence, they claim, 'illustrates how we can unfairly label a school as a poor performer when in fact it is doing rather well with a low achieving intake, and how an apparently high performing school is doing relatively badly when allowance is made for its high achieving intake.' These problems about evaluating a school's work are compounded by the Government's suggestion (DES, *National Curriculum: From Policy to Practice,* para 8.5) that the attainment of some pupils with special needs might be excluded from the published aggregate figures. Taken together, these considerations suggest that the true worth of a school will not be revealed in the published information on attainment in the National Curriculum.

Barry Stierer, in recognising that assessment is 'arguably the cornerstone of the 1988 Education Reform Act', notes that decisions are still awaited on a number of crucial issues. After outlining the framework for the system of national assessment as developed by the Task Group and since modified in certain respects, Stierer examines the concepts of formative and summative assessment. He concluded that assessment in the National Curriculum is essentially summative and as such is 'not therefore capable of providing the kind of detailed diagnostic information about individual pupils which can inform decisions about meeting children's educational needs'. Stierer discusses this fundamental criticism of the assessment arrangements in detail, and looks to records of achievement as a way of bridging the gap between what is required by the 1988 Act and what is meaningful for assessment and curriculum planning with pupils having special needs. Astonishingly, the statutory requirements for information to be included in the National Record of Achievement, launched by the Secretary of State in February 1991, are limited to achievements in the National Curriculum. Yet the extensive pilot work which has been done in this area has focused more on the formative aspects of record-keeping in the belief that standards are raised through involving pupils in discussion about their achievements and what the next steps should be. Fortunately, because of the considerable amount of research and development over the past few years, the majority of LEAs now have in place schemes for records of achievement which go beyond a final, summative report.

The speed at which the 1988 Education Reform Act was brought to the statute book made it inevitable that the original proposals would need to be reconsidered, not least in relation to special educational needs. Yet, as we go to press, there are plans for further changes which could increase the vulnerability of children with special needs to the experience of failure. A source of motivation and pride in one's work towards short-term goals will be reduced if the recently-developed graduated assessment schemes are no longer allowed to count towards GCSE. As a result, the success of schools in supporting the progress of children with special educational needs could be jeopardised and further efforts discouraged.

It seems likely that there will continue to be a number of key changes in the application of the Education Reform Act, some due to ministerial peccadilloes and preferences, others following a more pragmatic appraisal of what is sensible for education in this country. From time to time the goalposts will be moved and the rules of the game changed. This is not new in education, and those most likely to win from formal schooling will continue to prosper whatever the changes; it is the pupils with special educational needs that are in most danger of being the losers.

which was thought to be one of the consequences of their former role of dependency.

Perhaps the sharpest distinction between the old and the new ideologies is the view that fundamental to the education of children with special needs are the issues of civil rights and equal opportunities. The debate about equalising access to education irrespective of gender, ethnicity or social class has increasingly been extended to those who might be disadvantaged by a disability. Thus special education has not only become a broader educational concept, it has also become part of a broader social and political debate.

These characteristics of what is here depicted as reconstructed special education are generalised tendencies rather than concrete achievements. Their assimilation into policy and practice at LEA and school levels is far from uniform. Evidence about the implementation of the Education Act 1981 (Goacher et.al., 1988) showed that progress was slow as well as patchy and there were wide variations among LEAs, for instance, in the proportions of pupils formally identified as having special educational needs as well as in the percentages of these children integrated in mainstream schools. Nevertheless, the emergence of an alternative conceptual framework for special education is indisputable, it is reflected in numerous contributions to the recent literature on special education (e.g. Booth et.al., 1987, Dessent 1987, Thomas and Feiler 1988, Roaf and Bines 1989), in LEA policy statements from this period (e.g. ILEA 1985) and in details of initial and inservice training for teachers (Sayer and Jones, 1985; Hegarty and Moses, 1988; CNAA, 1990).

The ideological position supporting this framework is one which asserts that ensuring equal rights of access for all pupils, minimising differentiation, avoiding labelling and categorisation and bringing parents into partnership with teachers, has the potential to bring about far-reaching improvements in the education of children with special educational needs. Such modest reforms as can be claimed so far have been achieved in the absence of adequate funding and at a time when the education system has been under considerable strain from many conflicting pressures. What then are the prospects for the immediate future? Will it be possible to consolidate this new ideology which seeks to protect the rights of children with special needs, which facilitates integration and the establishment of whole-school policies?

The Education Reform Act 1988

One of the explanations for the 1981 Education Act's failure to live up to the promise of post-Warnock thinking was that the political and economic climate prevailing at the Act's birth was significantly different from that which prevailed during its gestation (Welton and Evans, 1986). The same interpretation holds good when one considers the likely fate of the new special education ideology in the wake of the Education Reform Act. The ideological conflicts this time, however, were stridently proclaimed not only

13

in the Act itself but in the way the then Secretary of State for Education, Kenneth Baker, dealt with responses from the educational world. The fact that he attempted to suppress the 20,000 replies to his 1987 consultation papers (Haviland, 1988) suggests that he saw the expert opinion of educationists as irrelevant to the Act's basic objective. It is difficult not to accept Brian Simon's conclusion that the Education Reform Act was as much concerned with the pursuit of political motives as with reforming the education system (Simon, 1988). Simon sees clear evidence for this in a statement by Mrs Thatcher:

> ... just as we have gained political support in the last election from people who had acquired their own home and shares, so we shall secure still further our political base in 1991-1992 by giving people a real say in education and housing.

(The *Independent* 19.7.87, cited in Simon 1988, page 12).

To this end the Act was designed to loosen the hold of LEAs on schools and recreate a hierarchical system of education justified in terms of 'variety' and 'choice'. These were manifestations of dogma from the radical right whose commitment to consumer-led public services provided the essence of the new policy. The Education Reform Act was part of the broader agenda aimed at replacing the welfare state with the enterprise society.

This political instrumentalism was justified on the grounds that it would improve the quality of education in state schools. Market forces would ensure that standards were raised, the shape of the education service would increasingly be determined by consumers — who are the parents (or voters), not children — schools would compete to attract the consumer and would be rewarded accordingly. Simon (ibid) again quotes a prime ministerial promise: 'Money will flow to the good schools and good headmasters' (*Daily Mail*, 13.8.87, cited in Simon (1988), page 11). Leaving aside its blatant sexism, this statement indicates that rewards and incentives are intended for schools which successfully meet the needs of the most powerful and vociferous consumers. Headteachers are put into the role of entrepreneurial managers, albeit under control from head office and under the watchful eye of governing bodies suitably stiffened by the inclusion of captains of industry and commerce.

It is legitimate to question whether, in the ethos created by a system such as this, the rights and needs of the most vulnerable and disadvantaged pupils will be sufficiently safeguarded. The continued progress towards the special education reforms pursued in the 1980s depends partly on the acceptability of the ideology which was their driving force. And it is plain to see that this conflicts fundamentally with key elements in the new Conservative education doctrine. Ensuring that all children have equal rights of access to education and minimising differentiation will not be aided by the adoption of consumerism and the creation of a hierarchy of schools; the avoidance of categorisation and labelling will be impeded by the stress on competition, and the aim of parents working in partnership with teachers is weakened by the notion of parents as consumers of teachers' services.

Considerable disquiet has been expressed about the likely impact of the new legislation upon integration. The fear that children with special needs will be marginalised in the new education system leads Blaine (1989) to predict a return to 'special groups for special children'. Swann (1989) considers the measures for formal modification or disapplication of the national curriculum as a form of segregation, statements of special educational needs becoming 'certificates of exemption'. This, Swann considers, points to a 'bleak segregated future for many children'. Willey (1989), a primary school headteacher, expresses concern about the hidden incentive in the Act to regard children with special needs as a disadvantage to a school's academic standing. A possible consequence of this, she believes, would be to

> undo the years of patient work among all professionals which has enabled pupils with special educational needs (whether with statements or not) to be welcomed, valued and well taught in mainstream schools. (page 136)

Added to these concerns are many wider-ranging reservations. There has probably never been such an overwhelmingly adverse reaction to a piece of educational legislation as that which greeted the Education Reform Act. The timing, the haste and the reluctance to consult were bitterly criticised (Haviland, op cit), while the political radicalism, the degree of centralised control, the philosophical inconsistencies and ideological contradictions were widely deprecated (Simon, op cit; Wragg, 1988; Bash and Coulby, 1989; Lawton, 1989)

Many specific measures in the original Bill provoked heated debate: the National Curriculum, the bench-mark testing, the erosion of LEA control, the demolition of the ILEA and so on. Among the issues which generated active lobbying was that of special educational needs. This resulted in two notable outcomes: the addition of sections in the Act which acknowledged the existence of children with special needs and the subsequent co- option of special educators into the National Curriculum Council and the Schools Examination and Assessment Council.

Is it possible today to be more optimistic about the future of special education and the continuation of the last decade's reforms? Gradually more is understood about the translation of the ERA rhetoric into practical policies and there are indications that the hard line originally promulgated by Mr Baker is being moderated as various working groups and pilot schemes have demonstrated the difficulty of producing acceptable practice out of some of the more dogmatic tenets of the Act.

Pressure from individuals and organisations representing groups of children with particular needs helped to ensure that those commissioned to carry out the ground work on the National Curriculum were aware of the potential threats to the education of these children. The Task Group on Assessment and Testing, for example, made it clear that the national assessment programme must be a flexible one and able to cope with the full range of ability and needs. Moreover it must be an integral part of the teaching-learning process, yielding information about individuals' strengths and weaknesses. It recognised the importance of preserving the self-esteem of pupils with special educational needs, recommending that the conduct of the tests should be such as to avoid the danger of their seeing themselves as failures (TGAT, 1988). Whether the new streamlined paper-and- pencil tests will undermine these objectives, remains to be seen. Reassuringly, however, the Curriculum Working Groups have each in turn strongly asserted the principle that all children should be included in the framework of the National Curriculum and that programmes of study must not be so rigid as to limit access for any pupil:

> Teachers should have flexibility to select experiences and approaches which are appropriate to the needs of differing groups of children from within the programmes of study, and to use the teaching methods best suited for their purposes. (NCC, 1988a, para 7.35).

Of the early guidelines published, the document on English (NCC, 1988b) went furthest in thinking through the implications of making the curriculum accessible to children with special needs. the authors recognised that some children may struggle to reach Level 1, but say that the fact that 'they have started down the curricular path should be acknowledged as a real achievement' (para 13.5) Children with physical disabilities and sensory impairments need assistance to communicate their achievements, they need extra resources and they need recognition. The very language used here represented a step forward, a step away from the prospect of exclusion and marginalisation which accompanied early perceptions of the impact of the National Curriculum on children with special needs.

A powerful counter to such a prospect is contained in *A Curriculum for All* (NCC, 1989a) a discussion document produced by a Special Educational Needs Task Group set up in February 1989. In a positive and unequivocal way this establishes a set of principles designed to ensure that the rights of children with special needs are not compromised by the introduction of the National Curriculum. The right for all children to a broad and balanced curriculum is again asserted, as is the need for a broad approach to defining needs.

In the same document strong support is given to the development of whole-school policies on special needs and to the use of co- operative teaching and flexible support systems. There is also an implicit recognition that heightened competitiveness in schools can work against the interests of those with special needs. The authors stress the importance of establishing a supportive environment:

> a climate of warmth and support in which self-confidence and self-esteem can grow and in which all pupils feel valued and able to risk making mistakes as they learn, without fear of criticism. (NCC 1989a, Section 2.4, page 8).

In fact this document could be seen as direct attempt to bring the reconstructed special education back into the frame, to encourage continuity in its development and resist the threats posed by certain elements in the Education Reform Act.

It should be said that not all aspects of the new legislation are inimical to the interests of children with special educational needs. The idea of a national curriculum accords well with the objective of normalising their education and ensuring access to the fullest possible range of subjects. Removing the divisions and distinctions between special and mainstream education has long been advocated, and the dialogue generated by the advent of the National Curriculum has assisted this. It has provided a common language for discussion of curriculum and attainment and has forced a good deal of re-thinking of traditional assumptions and ideas about the curriculum of children with special needs.

This book provides evidence of the progress being made in terms of the analysis and justification of their curriculum. A common curriculum makes transfer between schools less problematic so, notwithstanding the reservations mentioned earlier, the prospect for integration could in fact be enhanced. Archer (1989) has argued that the new curriculum framework will greatly ease the teacher's task of identifying appropriate learning experiences for integrated pupils.

Prospects for the future

Despite these signs that children with special educational needs may ultimately benefit from aspects of the new legislation, a number of serious threats remain. We still await the publication of numerous regulations, orders and circulars and no doubt we shall continue to see a mitigation of the apparent rigidity and dogmatism of the Act itself. The fact remains, however, that its underlying ideology is at odds with that which has come to be accepted as the proper basis for ensuring adequate and appropriate support for any child who needs it. While 'right of access' and flexibility' have now become indispensable elements in ministerial rhetoric — as shown in Alan Howarth's address to an NCSE conference in March 1990 — there are certain structural changes in the new system which are capable of thwarting such intentions. A consideration of five central measures in the Act reveals a number of unresolved issues. The measures concerned relate to the

National Curriculum, the arrangements for regular testing, opting out, the local management of schools and parental involvement.

i. The National Curriculum

It is ironic that protest about the absence of any reference to children with special needs in the original Bill should have led to the inclusion in the Act of sections which with hindsight seemed to have negative connotations. The sections by means of which the National Curriculum can be disapplied or modified theoretically allow for the blanket exemption of certain groups. This, for many, has raised the spectre of a return to the old concept of 'ineducability' which had only been excised from English education in 1970. In a system where education equates with pursuit of a centrally defined curriculum, those excluded from this are, by implication, ineducable. It now appears, however, that such measures would only be resorted to in extreme circumstances; the National Curriculum Council, for example, has supported minimal use of these exceptional arrangements (NCC, 1989b). Those concerned with the education of children with the most profound handicaps have interestingly led the way in exploring the potential of modification as opposed to disapplication (Ashdown, Carpenter and Bovair, 1991).

A different problem faces those responsible for pupils attending small units. A unit with 3.5 staff, twenty-five disaffected pupils and minimal facilities, for example, will have difficulty in offering a full curriculum. At present it is far from clear how this will be resolved. Disaffected pupils are not statemented — indeed the Education Act 1981 specifically excluded them from the requirement — so the statement cannot be used to prescribe an alternative curriculum. This difficulty might throw doubt on the future viability of small units, though, as will be seen, pressures from elsewhere in the 1988 Act may increase demand for such alternatives to normal schooling.

ii. Regular assessment

The proposals for national tests for all children at ages 7, eleven, fourteen and sixteen initially aroused considerable adverse reaction, not because of any aversion to regular formative assessment but because of what appeared to be a confused view of its purposes and uses. Rather than being seen as a part of the curriculum planning process or as a diagnostic aid, the original concept seemed to imply the measurement of children against national bench-marks and the production of a measure of individual schools' 'success'. The dangers in this have been thoroughly aired in the educational press, and pilot schemes have revealed a number of potential logistic and technical problems. This in turn has led to new regulations requiring slimmer, group-administered tests. However sensitively the new arrangements take account of the varying needs of children, problems are likely to arise because of the way results are regarded and used by teachers, parents, pupils, school governors and, possibly, the local press.

In a system in which reliance is placed on the marketing of education, the competitive ethos may give rise to a number of unintended consequences. One of these is that regular testing against what are seen as national norms of attainment will exacerbate the 'failure syndrome' which has bedevilled the progress of many children with learning difficulties. Given children's 'natural' proclivity towards competitiveness and given the average parent's anxiety over his or her child's progress, the heightened public profile given to the key stage assessments will make it more difficult to play down the labelling of pupils which inevitably follows. Even if it is only aggregated group scores which are open to public scrutiny, schools will need to find ways of conducting the assessment procedure and processing the results which will minimise threats to the self-esteem of some pupils.

iii. Opting Out

This measure gives schools the maximum opportunity to exploit the market economy ethos. One of the main objectives of Grant- Maintained School Status is to extend parental choice, mainly at the secondary level. Opted-out schools, together with City Technology Colleges (and the hybrid Arts Technology and Christian Technology Colleges) would constitute a new stratum in the education system between private schools and LEA schools. The hidden precondition for a school's elevation to this stratum will almost certainly be some degree of economic commitment on the part of parents. Opted-out schools will be for the children of parents who can afford to pay for extras, the CTCs, of course, receiving commercial sponsorship. Competition for entry will be fierce and some form of selection will inevitably take place. The result will be a three-tier education system like that anticipated by Campbell et.al. (1987), consisting of well- resourced private schools, state schools subsidised by their pupils' parents, and an underclass of LEA schools existing on minimal funding in areas of poverty.

The claim that the new tier of schools will extend freedom of choice for parents and raise standards in competing establishments is spurious. In practice, greater choice will be available only to the most socially privileged minority; and, while the standards in these schools are likely to be high, it will be through their ability to recruit the most able and advantaged pupils. Their competitors will not necessarily have access to equivalent resources and support. Wragg (1988) correctly predicted favourable treatment from the government, including government-funded publicity, in order to demonstrate the success of the policy. It is, he maintained, an example of a rigged market. The fact that the Grant-maintained School Trust, an allegedly independent, charitable body set up to encourage and help schools to opt out, is funded with government money, does nothing to weaken Wragg's argument.

The 1988 Act does contain some ostensible safeguards. Opted-out schools may not immediately change their character and must gain the

Secretary of State's approval when they eventually do so. In theory this policy gives an opportunity for minority groups to take greater control over the schools their children attend, a trend which would be welcomed by Campbell et.al. (1987) as an indication that our system could be more openly responsive to their needs than is possible with schools obliged to take a pluralist approach. Campbell et.al. also point out however, that the principle of community choice could also be used to pursue the ends of social and racial prejudice. Not only does open enrolment legitimise the removal of children from multi-ethnic schools but recruitment policies adopted by grant-maintained schools can similarly lead to the increased ghettoization of schooling.

It is easy to see how these same processes might work to the disadvantage of children with disabilities, learning difficulties or behaviour problems. Pupils with special needs who are not given the protection of a statement will be particularly vulnerable and there is a real prospect of deviant and less able children gradually being shunted downwards through the system into 'sink' schools. Thus the opting-out policy increases the risk of ascribing marginal status to children with special needs, making segregation more likely, perhaps in special units, or, as Brighouse (1989) predicts, making them 'doomed to grace and favour treatment... in division three schools'.

iv. Local management of schools

The delegation to schools of the direct management of their budgets has in the initial transition period proved to be one of the most complex and controversial policy changes in the Act. It is one of the essential ingredients in the market economy philosophy — schools operating on the lines of small businesses and able to respond more readily to the wishes of parents. The unsatisfactory nature of the initial funding formula has been widely demonstrated, for example, in relation to actual salary costs, where different schools have different budgetary demands according to the age profile of their teaching staff.

One of the most serious difficulties raised by LMS and yet to be resolved is that of covering the cost of responding to special needs among a school's population. At present the key funding variables are the numbers and ages of pupils on roll. Despite a widespread acceptance that the proportion of pupils with special educational needs varies widely between schools and districts, the funding formula has only the most crude of mechanisms to take account of this. The part of the formula relating to 'socio-economic needs' has proved to be difficult to interpret in practical terms. The use of pupils' post codes or the take-up of free meals as indices of special needs have obvious shortcomings and there is an urgent need for an alternative arrangement to be instituted. Willey (op.cit.) has argued for the establishment of an LEA contingency fund, additional to the general schools' budget. This would presumably be allocated on the basis of each school's identification of children who have a demonstrable need for extra support in order to gain maximum possible access to the National Curriculum.

Children who have statements of special educational needs are already supported from such a fund — somewhat grudgingly it might appear, since their provision is now subject to termly review. And cases have been reported of pressure upon mainstream school teachers to discourage them from instituting the statementing procedure. The LEA concerned presumably suspected them of using this as a device to make savings on the school's general budget.

Until problems and anomalies such as these have been resolved, local financial management would seem to be capable of damaging the education of children with special needs. Those without statements in particular might find themselves an unattractive proposition for mainstream schools: first because their SAT performance may reflect badly in the league table of results; secondly because modification and short-term disapplication of the National Curriculum will mean considerable extra work for already over-stretched staff; and thirdly because they may be seen as disproportionate consumers of limited financial resources.

v. Parental Power

It may seem paradoxical that while one of the cardinal features of the Education Reform Act is the degree of centralised control, it also has the aim of making parents more responsible for their children's education and giving them more scope to influence what goes on in schools. These latter objectives would not however be achievable without the exercise of strong state control, which is necessary to lessen the influence of LEAs and other power groups such as the teacher unions in order to make room for the operation of market forces. These are mediated through parents exercising their power as consumers of education, putting pressure on the providers to deliver a quality product.

In special education, where the value of parental involvement has long been appreciated, there is ample evidence that organised parental pressure has made a significant contribution to improvements in the care and education of children with special needs. This is particularly true of the low-incidence handicaps such as visual and hearing impairment, mental handicap and autism, which typically occur across the range of socio-economic groups. However, the increased reliance on parental pressure to ensure the quality of education becomes more problematic when one considers children with the high-incidence, non-normative handicaps — those with moderate learning difficulties. These represent no fewer than 60% of statemented children, and they come overwhelmingly from the lower socio-economic groups. The parents of these children are likely to be less able and motivated to assert their offsprings' rights. The same is true of the even larger number of pupils in mainstream schools, who, while not formally identified through the statementing process, attract the labels of 'slow learner', 'disruptive' or 'disaffected'.

The question which arises when a system increases the scope for parental influence, therefore, is — which parents? The likelihood is that parents of the more able and conforming children will be most likely to exercise their power, become involved in steering school policies, and influence local decisions about resource priorities. In this factor is taken in conjunction with the likely competition between schools to attract pupils and selectivity in school admission policies, then equality of access for all children does not seem so certain. Similarly when this factor is considered alongside the need for hard bargaining over a school's expenditure on costly specialist support services, then the evident danger arises that the recently improved systems of in-school support for children with special needs will not receive the level of resourcing they require.

From the point of view of those responsible for providing special education, whether in special schools or mainstream schools, and from the point of view of the children and young people receiving it (and their parents), the main advantage arising from the Education Reform Act will be the National Curriculum. As well as initiating an unprecedented amount of curriculum analysis, development and experimentation which is serving as a powerful stimulus to the whole education service, it will provide a much clearer framework for special educators and build stronger bridges between the special and mainstream sectors. It can only help in continuing efforts to escape from pre-Warnock criticisms about narrow, restricted and watered-down curricula offered to children with disabilities and learning difficulties. However, the crucial issue of ensuring access for all children depends not only on the refinement and integrity of the National Curriculum's design but on many other factors. Leaving aside the vexed question of providing sufficient resources to undertake such a massive operation (and the UK devotes less of its gross domestic product to education than most other developed countries: in 1987, 4.9 percent as compared with 6.7 percent in the USA, 7.2 percent in Sweden and 7.9 percent in Denmark), there are measures in the Education Reform Act itself, which, as has been shown, conspire against the interests of some children.

The agenda which special education took on in the 1980s remains uncompleted and great vigilance and determination will be required to ensure that the spirit of the 1981 Education Act survives the present upheaval.

References

Archer, M (1989) 'Targeting change', *Special Children,* No.33, pp.14-15.

Ashdown, R., Carpenter, B., and Bovair, K. (Eds.) (1991) *The Curriculum Challenge: pupils with severe learning difficulties and the National Curriculum.* Lewes; Falmer Press.

Bash, L. and Coulby, D. (1989) *The Education Reform Act: Competition and Control,* Cassell: London.

Blaine, R. (1989) 'A mystery in two acts', *Special Children,* No.31. pp.5-6.

Booth, T., Potts, P. and Swann, W. (Eds.) (1987) *Preventing Difficulties in Learning,* Oxford: Blackwell.

Brighouse, T. (1989) 'Effective schools and pupil needs', in Jones, N. and Southgate, T.(Eds.) *The Management of Special Needs in Ordinary Schools,* London: Routledge.

Campbell, J., Little, V., and Tomlinson, J. (1987) 'Multiplying the divisions? Intimations of educational policy post-1987', *Journal of Educational Policy* 2 (4), pp.369- 378.

Council for National Academic Awards (1990) *Review of Special Educational Needs in Initial and In-service Teacher Education Courses,* London: CNAA.

Department of Education and Science (1978) *Special Educational Needs.* (The Warnock Report), London: HMSO.

Dessent, T. (1987) *Making Ordinary Schools Special,* Lewes: Falmer Press.

Feiler, A. and Thomas, C. (1988) 'Special needs: past, present and future' in Thomas, G. and Feiler, A. (Eds.) *Planning and Provision for Special Needs,* Oxford: Blackwell.

Goacher, B., Evans, J., Welton, J., and Wedell, K. (1988) *Policy and Provision for Special Educational Needs,* London: Cassell.

Haviland, J. (Ed.) (1988) *Take Care Mr Baker!* London: Fourth Estate.

Hegarty, S. and Moses, D. (Eds.) (1988) *Developing Expertise: INSET for Special Educational Needs,* Windsor.

Inner London Education Authority (1985) *Educational Opportunities for All?* (The Fish Report), London: ILEA.

National Curriculum Council (1988a) *Science for Ages 5-16,* London: DES.

National Curriculum Council (1988b) *English for Ages 5-11,* London: DES.

National Curriculum Council (1989a) *A Curriculum for All,* York: NCC.

National Curriculum Council (1989b) *Circular 5: Implementing the National Curriculum — Participation by Pupils with Special Educational Needs.* York: NCC.

Roaf, C. and Bines, H. (Eds.) (1989) *Needs, Rights and Opportunities,* Lewes: Falmer Press.

Sayer, J. and Jones, N. (Eds.) (1985) *Teacher Training and Special Educational Needs,* Beckenham: Croom Helm.

Simon, B. (1988) *Bending the Rules — Baker's 'Reform' of Education,* London: Lawrence and Wishart.

Swann, W. (1989) 'The educational consequences of Mr Baker', *Special Education,* 13, pp.18-19.

Task Group on Assessment and Testing (1987) *The Report of the Task Group on Assessment and Testing,* London.

Welton, J. and Evans, J. (1986) 'The development and implementation of special education policy: where did the 1981 Act fit in?', *Public Administration,* 64 (2), pp.200-227.

Willey, M. (1989) 'LMS: a rising sense of alarm', *British Journal of Special Education,* 16 (4), pp.136-138.

Wragg, T. (1988) *Education in the Market Place,* London: NUT.

Chapter 2

Government Planning and Legislation for Special Needs

Margaret Peter

Since the passing of the 1988 Education Reform Act, two trends have been conspicuous in the secondary legislation, government circulars and pronouncements of education ministers. One is the loosening of the National Curriculum arrangements for pupils with special educational needs, the other is the tightening of plans for the local management of schools (LMS).

The gradual loosening of the stranglehold of the National Curriculum over what goes on in classrooms began, of course, before the Education Reform Bill sank exhausted onto the statute books in July 1988. during almost unprecedented hours of debate, and well in advance of the new curriculum's official launch into schools in September 1989. Clauses were added to the Bill to allow the National Curriculum to be modified or disapplied in a wider range of situations than first planned. The subject working groups' proposals for programmes of study and statements of attainment in the core subjects, published from August 1988 onwards, were also amended in order to avoid restricting access to pupils with certain learning difficulties and disabilities.

Critics who feared that pupils with special educational needs would be denied entry to the 'balanced and broadly based' curriculum which was supposed to be open to pupils in general, were also encouraged by the news towards the end of the year, that Dr Ronald Davie and Professor Peter Mittler, both identified with special educational needs, were being appointed, respectively, to the National Curriculum Council (NCC) and the School Examinations and Assessment Council (SEAC) and that a task group for special needs would shortly be formed. Early on, the National Curriculum Council had made clear its commitment to this area of education.

By March 1989, claims about the 'flexibility' of the National Curriculum from the Department of Education and Science were being reinforced by Circular 6/89 (*National Curriculum: Mathematics and Science Orders Under Section 4*). Paragraph 36 said that, provided a pupil was taught mainly the programme of study material within the levels appropriate to his or her key stage in the National Curriculum, schools could teach the pupil for part of the time at a level lower or higher than the key stage in question. Also, a pupil might be moved up or down a key stage for a particular subject to work with pupils who were older or younger 'where it makes sense and is practicable'. Circular 6/89 also seemed to be hinting at further flexibility: that the range of levels in the programme of study materials within the ranges should be taught to all, or even most, pupils within the key stage in question'. This could be reasonably interpreted as allowing teachers to pick and choose the material to be taught according to pupils' needs and the time available. So far, the Department of Education and Science, though uneasy about this interpretation, has not offered an alternative explanation.

By the time Circular 6/89 appeared, members of the National Curriculum Council task group on special needs had begun work on drafting the National Curriculum Council's first circular on special needs, *Implementing the National Curriculum — Participation by Pupils with Special Educational Needs,* and were beginning to plan their contribution to the Council's new *Curriculum Guidance* series. The Council had decided to give early priority to special educational needs in its publishing timetable through its Circular Number 5 and second booklet of curriculum guidance.

The Circular was published in May 1989, and *A Curriculum for All: Special Educational Needs in the National Curriculum* the following October. Both urged access and equal entitlement for pupils with special needs and sought the flexibility for this to happen. Through these publications the National Curriculum Council succeeded in promoting a slightly more liberal emphasis on National Curriculum accessibility than given in Circular 6/89. In a section in *A Curriculum for All* there was a contribution by the DES which referred to paragraph 36 of 6/89 mentioned above. The Department now stated, with a significant addition in brackets, that 'It will be possible for pupils to be taught for part of the time (perhaps as much as half or more) at levels below those specified for their key stage'... The option that pupils could be taught with younger pupils, through being held back and repeating a year, was discouraged by the National Curriculum Council as being one which would 'not often be practicable or educationally desirable...'

Another sign of increased official willingness to consider loosening up the National Curriculum for pupils with special needs came nearly a year later in the National Curriculum Council's Annual Report for 1989/90 which announced support for a curriculum project at Cambridge Institute of Education. One aim of the project was to 'develop additional statements of attainment in Level One', and another was to 'advise the Secretary of State on modification to Orders to provide greater access to the National Curriculum for pupils with severe, profound and multiple learning difficulties'. The project team's Curriculum guidance was published in March 1992 and one of the team's proposals on access has been reflected in Statutory orders.

At the same time as the National Curriculum was being re-examined to encourage greater access for pupils with special educational needs, the DES had begun to have second thoughts on other aspects of policy related to the National Curriculum. The introduction of individual curriculum plans for all pupils was quietly laid aside for a while, and the proposals of the Task Group on Assessment and Testing for teacher moderation in national assessments at key stages were judged impracticable. Concessions were made on the extent of standard assessment tasks (SATs) at Key Stage 1 and on the primacy of SATs' results over teacher assessments. The Statutory order for *Assessment Arrangements for English, Mathematics and Science* and related circular, issued in July 1990, provides that in certain circumstances, where a difference between the results of SATs and teacher assessments cannot be reconciled, teachers' judgements may be allowed to take precedence. Such differences may arise in particular, in relation to children who react emotionally to testing.

An outstanding example of the unravelling of the National Curriculum was the announcement in January 1991 by the Secretary of State, Kenneth Clarke, that the overloaded curriculum for 14 to 16 year-olds in Key Stage 4 being relaxed to allow more scope for vocational and other options outside the core and foundation subjects. Not all of the ten subjects previously envisaged for Key Stage 4 would now be compulsory. This would benefit those pupils in the last two years of statutory schooling who are most at risk of being alienated by a narrow and academic curriculum and of becoming disruptive. Earlier, in March 1989, the Elton report *Discipline in Schools* had acknowledged that the content and delivery of the curriculum were 'significant factors' associated with disruption.

While there has been a slackening of the National Curriculum arrangements, the grip of LMS has been getting tighter and more extensive. In December 1990 the Junior Education Minister for schools announced that local education authorities must delegate a higher percentage of the potential school's budget (85%) to schools by April 1993. Additionally, by April 1994, all maintained special schools must have delegated budgets too. The decision was made after the Department of Education and Science had received a report from Touche Ross, *Extending Local Management to Special Schools,* in October 1990, which saw the extension of total management to special schools as 'feasible and desirable' but recommended that the regulations should be enabling rather than mandatory.

In addition the Department of Education and Science put pressure on local education authorities to reduce the amount of money they hold centrally for discretionary exceptions which include the schools' psychological, peripatetic and advisory teacher services and other services to support children with learning difficulties and disabilities.

Fears about such changes were unlikely to have been dispelled when, at a conference run by The Spastics Society in October 1990 the then Secretary of State for Education, John MacGregor, dismissed as 'myths' the argument that limits on the money held by LEAs for spending on central services would prevent local authorities from making proper provision for pupils with special needs and the contention that governors should not be given responsibility for these pupils because they would fail to provide adequately for them. Some members of his audience may have wondered if they were listening to fairy tales as well as 'myths'.

The contrast in these two trends, tightening the grip with one hand and loosening the stranglehold with the other, is not surprising. If the National Curriculum is seen by the Government as an instrument for encouraging market forces, providing a convenient shopping guide for parents looking for the 'best buys' in schools, it will need to be preserved as far as possible. Faced, however with an exhausted teaching force, shortages of qualified staff for some core and foundation subjects, lowered staff morale, resignations and other setbacks the DES needs to make just enough concessions to retain teachers' co-operation and to prevent the National Curriculum from disintegrating. At the same time market forces can flourish more strongly if schools are delegated the maximum amount of money that LMS will allow and that they can spend, within limits, as they choose.

The consequences of these two simultaneous trends are difficult to predict. One possibility is that in the longer term, relaxation in the National Curriculum arrangements will mean that more children with special needs will stay in the mainstream without having any special provision for their needs protected by statements under the 1981 Education Act. In the short term, however, the percentage of children with statements has begun to rise. Fear of a 'significant increase' in the number of statements runs high at the DES, though a curiously ambivalent attitude was revealed in Circular 22/89. On the one hand, it discouraged statementing through its reference to a court ruling about an LEA's option to leave schools to make provision rather than issuing a statement under the 1981 Education Act. On the other hand, several paragraphs later, there was the suggestion that National Curriculum assessments might help to identify more pupils with special needs — a proportion of whom would almost inevitably be seen as requiring statements under Section 5 of the 1981 Act.

The tightening of the LMS requirements is likely to reduce further the support available to non-statemented pupils with special needs in ordinary schools. The numbers of learning support and other peripatetic and advisory teachers have already been reduced in some local authorities, and school governors may give low priority to special educational provision.

One reaction to this situation from mainstream teachers, parents and governors with tepid commitment to special educational provision but anxious about competition from nearby schools, will be to look to streaming, setting and even holding some children back to repeat a year. They may also try covertly to avoid admitting such pupils under open enrolment. Meanwhile grant-maintained schools are being encouraged by the Government to become grammar schools. Strategies like these could help to rescue teachers from the demands of a wide ability range as well as from the risk of published results that compare unfavourably with those of other schools when pupils are assessed nationally at the key stages. Warnings about a wide scale return to a selective system of education have been rife ever since the publication of the Education Reform Bill in November 1987.

If this movement towards wider divisions between schools is to be contained, if not reversed, a key priority will be to improve schools' ability to match teaching to individual needs — 'differentiation' as the current jargon has it. Surveys from Her Majesty's Inspectorate such as *A Survey of Pupils with Special Educational Needs in Ordinary Schools* (December 1989) and *Provision for Primary Aged Pupils with Statements of Special Educational Needs in Mainstream Schools* (February 1990) point out that in too many schools, work is not matched closely enough to pupils' varying needs.

Recent projects have begun to tackle this problem. Reports on classroom practice include *Differentiation in Action* from the National Foundation for Educational Research and *Differentiation in the Primary School* from the Northern College of Education, Scotland. In-service training materials have come from the Open University, the London University Institute of Education, voluntary organisations, like the recently formed National Association for Special Educational Needs, and many local education authorities. The National Curriculum Council is also interested in the theme of differentiation.

Initiatives like these show promise, and more are needed. In the long run, however, the prospect for schools in the confusion of continuing change, may have little to do with the DES plans to tighten or loosen its grip. Losing it could be the real issue.

Chapter 3

Local Management of Schools and Special Educational Needs

Jennifer Evans and Ingrid Lunt

The Law

The Education Reform Act of 1988 has changed radically the way schools are financed. This is achieved through local management of schools (LMS). The intention behind this initiative is to delegate as much responsibility to schools as possible, with a limited number of services provided centrally by the LEA — but only where this is shown to be more efficient or effective. According to DES Circular 7/88 on LMS:

> Local Management of Schools represents a major challenge and major opportunity for the education service. The introduction of needs-based formula funding and the delegation of financial and managerial responsibilities to governing bodies are key elements in the Government's overall policy to improve the quality of teaching and learning in schools.

Sections 33 and 55 of the Act cover financial delegation. Originally this applied to all secondary schools, while primary schools with less than 200 pupils were exempt unless the local education authority chose (as some did) to give them delegated budgets. New DES regulations, explained in Circular 7/91, extend LMS to all primary schools, regardless of size, by April 1994.

The Act had also empowered the Secretary of State to extend LMS to special schools, and the Government subsequently commissioned a detailed feasibility study by Touche Ross Management Consultants.

Following the recommendations of the Touche Ross Report, the Secretary of state announced his intention to issue regulations in order to include in the LMS scheme those special schools which desire it. Nursery schools, however, are still excluded.

Under Section 33 of the 1988 Act, LEAs prepare schemes of financial delegation for the Secretary of State, who may improve the proposals, turn them down, modify them, or impose his own scheme if the LEA's is considered unsuitable. After a local authority scheme has been approved by the Secretary of State, it has to be published (Section 42) before the beginning of the financial year. Details have to include:

- the amount of the 'general schools budgets' (GSB), i.e. the total LEA spending on schools

- the amount of the 'aggregated schools budgets' (ASB), i.e. the part of the GSB which is to be delegated

- the amount and nature of 'excepted items', i.e. those retained by the LEA

- details of the allocation formula

- the planned expenditure per pupil in each school covered by the scheme

- expenditure per pupil on excepted (i.e. not delegated) services

At the end of the financial year, LEAs are required to publish a report on expenditure actually incurred during the year.

DES Circulars 7/88 and 7/91 set out the timescale over which LMS is to be implemented, offer guidance, and outline criteria for schemes of management.

Delegated items

LEAs are expected to delegate the large majority of expenditure on schools, including:

- salary costs of teaching and non-teaching staff

- schools' day-to-day premises costs, includes rates and rent, repairs and maintenance

- books, equipment and other goods and services used by the schools.

Mandatory exceptions

As DES Circular 7/91 explains, there are now two items of expenditure which are 'mandatory exceptions', i.e. they must be kept under LEA control:

- capital expenditure on schools
- specific government and EC grants (e.g. Section 11, TVEI, Travellers' Children)

Discretionary exceptions

Additionally, there are a number of discretionary exceptions which LEAs may except from delegation if they so wish. These are:

- inspectors/advisers
- home-to-school transport
- pupil support
- peripatetic/advisory teachers
- LEA initiatives
- structural repairs/maintenance
- statemented pupils/special needs
- psychologists
- education welfare officers
- school-specific contingencies
- library and museum services
- premises and equipment insurance
- special staff costs
- school meals
- governors' insurance
- dismissal and premature retirement costs
- transitional excepted items (until April 1993).

Originally, the total amount spent by the LEA on items excepted from delegation was restricted to no more than 10 percent of the General Schools Budget (GSB). However, the DES now regards the GSB as an inappropriate basis for delegating budgets, and has introduced a new criterion called the Potential Schools Budget (PSB). The PSB excludes expenditure on certain large items, viz, capital, special grants (such as Section 11 payments), home-to-school transport, school meals, and money used to facilitate transition to LMS. The new ruling requires LEAs to allocate to schools at least

85 percent of the PSB by April 1993 (1995 for Inner London authorities). The PSB minus the excepted items becomes the Aggregated Schools Budget (ASB) which is distributed to schools according to a formula to become each school's budget share or delegated budget.

The Formula

The original regulations, explained in Circular 7/88, required that at least 75 percent of the ASB be allocated to schools on the basis of pupil numbers weighted only for age: but more recent regulations, explained in Circular 7/91, increased this to a minimum of 80 percent from April 1993 (1995 in London), a requirement which in practice most LEAs were satisfying already. However, in addition to age, it is now also possible for LEAs to give weightings within the 80 percent limit for pupils with special educational needs, whether or not they have statements (and also for pupils in designated nursery classes).

Each LEA is expected to devise its own formula, having regard to local needs and circumstances, but observing the following principles:

1. It should be simple, clear and predictable.

2. It should be based on an assessment of schools' objective needs, rather than on historic patterns of expenditure.

3. In spite of the facility for special needs weightings explained above, the central determinant should be the numbers of pupils in each school, weighted for difference in their age to yield age-weighted pupil units or AWPU).

4. It should include two other specific factors:

    a. variations in the additional costs of pupils with special educational needs which is counted against the 20 percent *not* allocated on the basis of AWPU;

    b. different subject weightings within sixth form provision.

Optionally, LEAs may also include certain other factors in the formula:

1. variations in the salary costs of small schools

2. non-statutory special needs, e.g. social deprivation

3. area of premises

4. type of premises

5. condition of premises

6. other premises factors, e.g. vandalism, special facilities).

There is a transitional period of four years to run from the date of introduction of an approved scheme in order to moderate the speed of adjustment from historic to formula funding. After the transitional period,

LEAs may limit changes in schools' budgets between years to 5 percent in constant prices.

The Intention Behind LMS

The intention of the 1988 Act is to raise standards and make schools more responsive to their clients — parents, pupils, the local community and employers — and to local needs:

> The Government has presented... a package, designed to promote accountability and responsiveness of schools and the LEAs to their consumers. (Coopers & Lybrand, 1987)

Local Management of Schools and the delegation of budgets to schools by means of a formula is a central element in this 'package':

> The funding of all the schools in a local authority area by means of a single formula is central to the strategy and ideology underlying the Act... and... it represents a stepping-stone for a possible future move to vouchers. (Maclure, 1989)

For many, 'LMS is best understood as creating a system of educational vouchers in our schools' (Thomas, 1990), an idea proposed by Sir Keith Joseph who, when Secretary of State for Education, claimed the need for increased parental choice. If it is possible to quantify the cost of the education of pupils at different ages (and with different needs?), and if schools receive resources mainly according to their pupil numbers, the logic goes, then schools will improve in order to attract parental choice.

The logic is disarmingly and misleadingly simplistic. It assumes either an unrealistic uniformity or the justification of harsh inequality or 'rough justice' between schools. As Willey (1989) comments:

> The notion of a school with control over its resources to meet the school's particular circumstances seems on the surface to be an educationalist's ideal.

However, as Willey also notes, when one considers the nature of the formula and the way in which schools are to receive their budgets, this ideal is in danger of being shattered:

> Drawing up a suitable formula is going to be extremely difficult. It will be difficult technically, because authorities will discover that costs differ widely from one school to another under present arrangements. These 'historic' differences may be simply the result of arbitrary decisions in the past. In many cases, however, these differences are not arbitrary anomalies, but reflect genuine differences in circumstances and the ways in which these have been met over the years. If they are simply swept away, some schools will be placed in an intolerable position by LMS.

LMS and children with special educational needs

Within schools, the allocation of resources to children should reflect their different educational needs. As far as children with special educational needs are concerned, their entitlement to educational resources is placed within the 1981 Act. Klaus Wedell (1989) has summarised clearly the main points arising from the 1981 Act in relation to the education of children with special educational needs:

> Special educational needs occur across a continuum of degree, because they are the outcome of the interaction between the strengths and weaknesses of the child, and the resources and deficiencies of the child's environment.

> It is therefore not meaningful to draw a clear dividing line which separate the 'handicapped' from the 'non- handicapped'.

> All children are entitled to be educated. The aims of education are the same for all children, but the means by which the aims can be attained differ, as does the extent to which they may be achieved.

> All schools have a responsibility to identify and meet children's special educational needs, and all children should be educated with their peers as long as their needs can be met and it is practicable to do so.

This formulation of special educational needs recognises the relativity of the definition stated in the Warnock Report (DES, 1978). Further, the Warnock Committee drew attention to the now well-known fact that about 20 percent of children would experience difficulty in learning and require some form of provision at some time in their school career. It is also well- known that, of these, on average 2 percent will be found in special schools and 18 percent in mainstream schools, with or without statements and with or without specific support. Unfortunately, the 1981 Act was passed and implemented without extra resources, and 'England thus became the only developed country to attempt special educational reform without an allocation of additional funds to carry it out' (Wedell, 1989).

The 1981 Act v. the 1988 Act

There are obvious conflicts between some of the principles of the 1981 Act and the intentions of the 1988 Act. The allocation of resources by age-weighted pupil units and parental choice may conflict with the necessity to provide extra resources for children with special educational needs. The identification and description of children's needs is a complex task which needs to take into account the relative and interactive nature of special educational needs which lie along a continuum from greater to lesser need. Some LEAs might be tempted to return to the pre-1981 Act categories in order to define need and to differentiate between the amount of extra resources required for children with different types of need. However, this would be to ignore the important contribution of the interaction between the child and the learning environment which contributes to the special educational need, and would leave out consideration of classroom and school factors which are well-known to make a difference. This issue has been thoroughly explored by Brahm Norwich (1990). There is also, as Russell (1990) suggests, the danger of 'a return to special schools as sanctuaries for resources and serious backtracking in ordinary schools where children with special needs may seem too expensive and complicated to manage.'

Protecting resources for children with special educational needs

The phenomenon of 'resource drift', mentioned by Tony Dessent (1987), will be increasingly difficult to prevent as schools face the problems involved in managing their own budgets and are permitted to hire funds and encouraged to make savings. The money delegated to schools for children without statement cannot be earmarked. If children with special educational needs, with or without statements, bring with them considerable extra resources, how will these be protected? If they bring with them smaller resource increase, what will be the school's incentive to take on such pupils? Russell (1990) has pointed out that 'many parents and professionals fear that children with special needs may seem less attractive to ordinary schools without the advocacy and support of coherent whole-authority policies and the relevant support and advisory services'. Further, as critics such as Willey (1989) have suggested, 'the hidden agenda of the Education Reform Act encourages the idea that pupils with special educational needs are a disadvantage to a school's academic results and, very importantly, to its use of teaching resources'.

In order to identify, quantify and earmark resources, schools may be tempted to increase the number of children put forward for statements of special educational need. The proportion of children with statements has always varied considerably across the country. The number of children with statements depends on several factors, including LEA policy (particularly that on resourcing), LEA provision, schools' ability to meet a wide range of pupils' needs, and the nature of pupils' special educational needs. Statements have often been the only way for a school to secure extra resources, and they may therefore sometimes have been used inappropriately. Furthermore, this way of allocating resources encourages an individualistic approach to meeting special needs and ignores the potential for whole-school or whole-authority approaches. There is the danger that headteachers may deliberately get more children statemented in order either to get more resources or to have children sent to a special school:

> Statements could increasingly be used to procure 'special resources'
> no longer forthcoming in a locally managed ordinary school system,

37

or, alternatively, the removal from the ordinary school of an 'expensive to educate' child whose learning outcomes might be seen as doing little to enhance the schools' public image'. (Dessent, 1989)

Most LEAs are retaining the statementing process (and provision to meet this) centrally, though clearly this budget is cash-limited. Some LEAs, however, are delegating statementing expenditure, and this will raise all kinds of issues for schools which are already under pressure to save money.

In summary, then, there are a number of issues within special educational needs provision which have been made more complicated by LMS:

1.   Governing bodies have a duty under the 1981 Act to ensure that the needs of pupils with special educational needs are met. This sometimes requires extra resources.

2.   Because the formula for delegating budgets to schools has to be 'simple, clear and predictable', the criterion for determining the special needs element is likely to be either numbers of free school meals or results in an LEA screening test. It is unlikely to be able to represent the complexity and interactive nature of special educational needs.

3.   The consequences of extending LMS to special schools will need careful monitoring.

4.   For the majority of LEAs, the statementing procedure is the main way of earmarking extra resources for pupils with special educational needs in special or ordinary schools. It is difficult to see how for many LEAs this will not lead to an increase in the number of statements. Our survey of a sample of LEAs for 1990-91 showed an average of around 2.4 percent compared with 2 percent the previous year — an increase which is only partly accounted for by a reduction in the proportion of children being educated in special schools.

5.   Many LEAs and schools have over the past few years developed whole-school policies and whole-authority policies to meet special educational needs. These have often depended on collaboration between schools and support services. LMS places schools in competition with each other and delegates many of the LEA support resources to schools, thereby making vulnerable authority-wide support services.

6.   The phenomenon of 'resource-drift' and the possibility of hirement means that schools will be forced to prioritise expenditure under different budgets heads. This may mean that provision for special educational needs is given low priority in comparison with some other headings.

7.   The formula for allocating budgets individualises 'need' and removes pupils from the learning context. If the continuum of need is to be adequately represented without a return to the pre-1981 Act categories, this would necessitate an enormously complicated formula and considerable expenditure on special educational needs by an LEA. Neither of these is necessarily possible or, in the first case, appropriate. Costing provision may be a laudable aim, but it is extremely complicated in the case of children with special educational needs.

8.   If the procedure for statementing (which in itself is expensive) is used as a resourcing mechanism, both delegation and non-delegation of statementing carry with them considerable difficulties.

9.   The package of reforms involving the National Curriculum, open enrolment, financial delegation and the publication of performance indicators such as National Curriculum assessment and GCSE results, means that schools will be competing against each other, parents choosing the school which offers the 'best' education. It is not clear where children with special educational needs fit into this package or how their needs will be met adequately within mainstream schools.

Early indications of the likely effects of LMS on special needs provision

In order to assess the range of responses to special educational needs within the scheme of financial delegation, we surveyed all English LEAs in Autumn 1989, on behalf of the University of London Institute of Education. Part of the questionnaire was designed to collect data on LEAs' plans for resourcing special provision under LMS.

Some 54 questionnaires were returned — 14 (26 percent) from London boroughs, 16 (30 percent) from metropolitan boroughs and 24 (44 percent) from shire counties. This represents 57 percent of all English LEAs. Shire counties and London boroughs were slightly over-represented in the sample, and the metropolitan boroughs slightly under-represented.

Discretionary exceptions

All the LEAs responding to the questionnaire had opted to retain central control over support services such as educational psychologists and peripatetic support teachers. The findings suggest that, with an increase in the proportion of funds to be delegated, it is the authorities with large support services that will be hardest hit. LEAs with large support teams tend to have fewer children with statements — presumably because the additional support for them is already available. A cut-back in support services is therefore likely to mean more statements in those LEAs. For LEAs which have already delegated most discretionary items of expenditure, an expansion of central services is virtually impossible unless there is an expansion in the schools budget.

Given these problems, and faced with shortfalls arising from the government's estimate of the amount of money LEAs need to spend on their services and raise through local taxation, it is unlikely that local authorities will be able to expand their special needs services in the near future. Consequently an LEA wishing to provide more support in mainstream schools, whether for statemented or non-statemented pupils, is going to have problems with resourcing.

The percentage of the school budget retained for discretionary exceptions was found to range from 5 percent to 10 percent, with most LEAs preparing for further cuts. Those keeping the largest proportions were not necessarily those with the largest number of educational psychologists or advisory teachers. As can be seen from Table 3.1 very few authorities were preparing to delegate special needs services.

Table 3.1. Services delegated by LEAs in 1989	
Service	**Number of Authorities N = 54 Delegating**
Educational Psychologists	0
Provision for statemented children in mainstream schools	2
Units in mainstream schools	9
Education welfare	1
Home Tuition	1

The formula

As explained earlier, the LMS regulations prescribe that a minimum proportion (originally at least 75 percent) of the aggregated schools budget must be allocated on the basis of age-weighted pupil units (AWPU). Beyond this proportion, LEAs can add to their formula weightings for such items as small schools, special educational needs, and other factors which might effect staffing ratios. As can be seen from Table 3.2 most LEAs in our sample added a 'special needs' weighting to their formula.

Table 3.2 also shows that ten LEAs (18 percent) did not have a special needs weighting for children without statements in their formula. Of those that did, the most common basis for allocating funds was the number of children on free school meals (Table 3.3). Over half the LEAs were pro-

Table 3.2 LEA Formula and SEN		
Proportion of budget allocated on AWPU	Number of LEAs	No. SEN Weighting
75%	10	1
76-79%	20	3
80-85%	20	6
85%+	1	

posing to use this criterion alone or in combination with some assessment of reading attainment. However, many acknowledged that this was an imperfect method. For one thing, it equates special educational needs with poverty. For another, the rules governing entitlement to free school meals are subject to variations, and are not the best method for measuring poverty. This reliance on the free meals criterion indicates the inadequacy of LEAs' information about the incidence of special needs within their mainstream schools.

Table 3.3 Basis for allocation of extra support	
	Number of LEAs
No SEN weighting	10
SEN weighting — free school meals only	21
SEN weighting — free school meals + tests	6
SEN weighting — reading assessment	7
SEN weighting — based on historic funding	2
SEN weighting — basis unknow	1
SEN weighting — National Curriculum Assessment	1
No response	6

On the question of whether to give delegates budgets to special schools, the LEAs were divided. One third said definitely no, one third said yes and one third were undecided. Shire counties were more likely to have delegated, while metropolitan boroughs were most likely to have rejected the idea.

This overall picture indicates that most authorities were attempting to protect provision for special educational needs by funding it centrally and being cautious about handing over resources to schools. At the same time, many were endeavouring to target extra funds more effectively towards schools which have significant proportions of children with special needs.

Three LEA case studies

At a recent conference held at the Institute of Education in London, representatives of three LEAs — Leeds, Cleveland and Berkshire — gave details of their contrasting approaches.

1. Leeds

Leeds has a strong commitment to meeting the needs of pupils with special educational needs, and this is reflected in the allocation of a substantial budget. At the time, this budget consisted of £5.8m, of which £3.7m was for additional staffing to support pupils with statements in mainstream schools and £2.1m was for pupils with special needs but without statements. It was proposed to delegate the £5.8m to schools on the following basis:

a. Schools would be allocated a minimum base budget for special needs, irrespective of the number of pupils with statements.

b. Statements would be allocated a number of 'units of SEN' in a manner which reflects the level of resourcing required to meet the provision required.

c. The 'units of SEN' could be increased or decreased in monetary terms in relation to the total number of units in the system and the budget set by the authority.

The statements had been allocated a number of 'units of SEN' according to four categories:

Category	Resource Implications	Number of units
A	Small group work, small amounts of individual teacher or nursery nurse time	1
B	Half-time nursery nurse or NTA or greater amounts of individual teacher time	5
C	Full-time NTA, full-time nursery nurse, substantial amounts of teacher time, up to half time	10
U	Support for pupils in specially resourced schools for pupils with emotional and behavioural difficulties and severe learning difficulties	25 for 1st pupil, then as described below

Age of pupil	Method of identification
5+	Infant screening scale
7+	LEA reading screening test
9+	LEA reading screening test
13+	Standardised reading test

Approximately 1,200 such pupils had been identified, and it had been decided to resource the schools in which these children were placed by using the category A criterion used for children with statements.

The *resourced schools and units* mentioned above had been funded on the basis of a pupil-teacher ratio of 1-7 for pupils with emotional and behavioural difficulties and for language difficulties, and on the basis of 1-6 for pupils with severe learning difficulties. The first pupil attracts 25 units (i.e. enough to buy a full-time teacher and NTA or nursery nurse). The next six pupils attract nothing. Then the eighth and every following seventh pupil attract 25 units. Thus as the numbers grow, so do the resources.

One advantage of this system is that it addresses the overlap between those children with mild learning difficulties who have statements and those who do not. It is also likely that such a system will reduce pressure on the LEA to make statements for children who need this level of resource since it should be forthcoming without the necessity for a statutory statement.

The Leeds solution is an ingenious way of financing support on a scale which would be prohibitive under 'discretionary exceptions'. It also gives the LEA the freedom to continue the move towards mainstream placement.

2. Berkshire

Berkshire has a substantial number of support services which would be difficult to resource centrally within their 7 percent 'discretionary exceptions' bank. At the time of the conference the LEA had 48 on-site and nine off-site units, 60 support teachers, 19.3 educational psychologists and 15.2 education social workers. The total cost of this provision was £4.8m. The intention was to delegate part of this resource to schools, retaining some centrally and allowing schools to buy in over and above the services delegated. This would affect educational psychologists and home tutors.

The authority planned to give extra resources to schools under the 25 percent of the aggregated schools budget which is not age-weighted pupil units, and to do this by using two indices: a Social Needs Index (50 percent of funding) and an Educational Needs Index (50 percent of funding).

The Social Needs Index is calculated on the basis of entitlement to free school meals. The amount given rises more steeply the more there are children entitled to free meals.

The Educational Needs Index is calculated according to the number of pupils at stages 2 and 3 of the authority's assessment procedures. Stage 2 is where the child's difficulties are discussed with a special needs teacher and progress will be monitored and evaluated. Stage 3 is where the school involves an outside agency such as the psychological services or the special needs support team, and special provision is made within the school. Again, there is a sliding scale, so that the more children a school has with special needs, the more steeply the amount of resource rises.

One problem with delegating the discretionary items is that schools may decide not to use funds for the purpose of buying in support. Berkshire intends to monitor this through its advisory service. However, since the funds allocated through age-weighted pupil units are so inflexible, there will always be pressure on schools to subsidise their budgets from special educational needs or other delegated discretionary exceptions.

3. Cleveland

Cleveland has a school population of 92,000. It has 16 special schools and 56 units, and there is a policy of integration wherever possible. The authority has 19.3 educational psychologists and 71 education social workers.

The high level of resources, particularly in relation to special units, meant that it would have been difficult to retain the funding for all special needs provision within the authority's 10 percent limited discretionary exceptions. Consequently, Cleveland decided that the costs of funding the units would be fully delegated, except in the case of units for pupils with sensory difficulties. In the latter, staffing would be provided from central services, but all other costs delegate. Formula-funding for each unit, which is calculated in January each year, is based on the estimated maximum number of pupils on roll in the following financial year.

The following services remain centrally funded: learning support, outreach support for children with learning difficulties in special schools, individual pupil support, pupils with visual difficulties, pupils with hearing difficulties, behaviour support, offsite units for disruptive pupils, additional specialist materials, initiatives, educational psychologists and education social workers.

In effect, Cleveland delegates the budgets for special units attached to mainstream schools (though only in part for pupils with sensory difficulties), but maintains central control of services and individual support.

Conclusions

There are a number of problems facing LEAs as they grapple with the dilemmas thrown up by LMS in relation to special educational needs.

First, although the day conference demonstrated a great commitment among the participants to resourcing pupils with special educational needs and to making creative use of the formula, the criterion used by the great

44

majority of LEAs to define special needs was the crude measure of free school meals.

Secondly, it is difficult to see how LEAs can ensure that money allocated to schools for special needs is in fact spent in this area. The survey showed a great variety of responses to the questions about the LEAs were proposing to resource pupils with special educational needs, and this was further highlighted in the three case studies outlined above.

The third problem relates to the retention of centrally-funded services. Most support services, including educational psychology, remain in the list of central services. Some LEAs, however, appear to be thinking in terms of retaining a skeleton service to carry out statutory duties and minimal LEA work, while delegating to schools the remainder of the budget for support services, such as educational psychologists. This will mean that it will be difficult to maintain a coherent LEA policy for children with special educational needs and impossible to ensure equal access to provision across schools in the LEA. Schools may find themselves under such pressure for expenditure under other heads, that buying in support services becomes a low priority.

It is still unclear what it would mean to delegate the statementing procedure (i.e. the cost of full assessment) or provision. The survey showed a wide range of percentages of statements between LEAs. Yet if a statement is to be used for identifying need and allocating resources, how will delegation ensure that resources are provided and properly used, and will it cope with the uneven distribution of statements across schools?

Lastly, the position of special schools, which are now to be given delegated financial management if they wish, remains problematic. Outside LMS, the necessity to make full and efficient use of resources might lead LEAs to place more pupils with special needs in special schools; inside LMS, it is not clear how the principle of attracting pupils through formula-funding would make sense in the case of special schools.

It will be essential to monitor how children with special educational needs fare under LMS, and in particular how the special needs of children in mainstream schools who do not have statements are to be provided for. The present authors intend to continue to monitor the position and to undertake further surveys and arrange national conferences.

References

Coopers and Lybrand (1987) *Local Management of Schools: A Report to the DES,* London: HMSO.

Department of Education and Science (1978) *Children and their Special Educational Needs,* (Warnock Report), London: HMSO.

Dessent, T. (1987) *Making the Ordinary School Special,* Lewes: Falmer Press.

Dessent, T. (1989) To 'statement' or not to 'statement' (editorial), *British Journal of Special Education,* Vol.16, No.1.

Maclure, S. (1989) *Education Re-formed,* London: Hodder and Stoughton. 2nd Edition.

Norwich, B. (1990) 'Decision-making about special educational needs', in Evans, P. and Verma, V. (Eds.) *Special Education: Past, Present and Future,* Lewes: Falmer Press.

Russell, P. (1990) 'The Education Reform Act: The implications for special educational needs', In Flude, M. and Hammer, M. (Eds.) *The Education Reform Act 1988: Its Origins and Implications,* Lewes: Falmer Press.

Swann, W. (1988) 'Trends in special school placement: Measuring, assessing and explaining segregation'. *Oxford Reveiw of Education, Vol.14, No.2.*

Thomas, H. (1990) 'From LFM', in Flude, M. and Hammer, M. (Eds.) *The Education Reform Act 1988: Its Origins and Implications,* Lewes: Falmer Press.

Touche Ross Management Consultants (1990) *Extending Local Management to Special Schools — A Feasibility Study for the Department of Education and Science,* London: HMSO.

Wedell, K. (1989) 'Children with special educational needs: past, present and future', In Evans, P. and Varma, V. (Eds.) *Special Education: Past, Present and Future,* Lewes: Falmer Press.

Willey, M. (1989) 'LMS: A rising sense of alarm', *British Journal of Special Education.* Vol.16, No.4.

Chapter 4

The Governor's Role in Special Needs in the Mainstream School

Deborah M. King

Introduction

This chapter looks at some of the changes in the governor's role and responsibilities which have taken place over the last twelve years. It asks how such changes affect the sizeable group of children with special educational needs in mainstream schools and attempts to delineate the responsibilities of the governors to those pupils. In particular the growth of parental influence in the governing bodies and in the field of special needs is considered, the introduction of the National Curriculum, and the governors' responsibility for the financial administration of schools.

Recent changes for the Governors' responsibilities towards special needs.

The last 15 years have brought considerable changes to the role of the governors; the nature of governors' meetings has changed; the number of meetings in most schools must have increased drastically, if only to deal with the new legislation. At the same time, although governors may feel swamped by the amount of legislation bringing such changes in their role, they must be aware that the concept of special educational need has changed: the Warnock Report effectively brought the discussion of special needs out of the special school and into the mainstream. Governors of all schools must be concerned with those children who at one time or another have special educational needs.

How do these changes in the role of the governor and the concept of special need interact? Where do the new responsibilities of the governor affect this sizeable group of children, their parents, and the school staff? In both areas parents have gained more right to be heard and the phrase 'parents as partners' has become popular. Governing bodies are more representative of the parents, and have gained more specific responsibilities especially in the area of the curriculum and over the school's budget. In the field of special education this period has also seen a change in the concept of special educational need and parental influence. The Warnock Report (DES, 1978) broadened the group of children who may need help or support at some time; it may be estimated that as many as 18 percent of pupils in mainstream schools need some sort of learning support, whether temporary or permanent. Here too, it was recommended that parents be given more power, and be seen as partners in education. The Warnock Report also recommended that children with special educational needs be integrated into mainstream education (with important caveats). The legislation of the 1980s has increased the governors' responsibilities in the mainstream school, and it has pointed out their responsibility in the process of integration of children with special educational needs. It has given them the oversight of the delivery of a broad and balanced curriculum to all pupils (in the great majority of cases this will be the National Curriculum); and the legislation has given governors the power, in theory, to determine priority areas of spending. School budgets will, for the most part, be administered by governing bodies in the 1990s.

Governing Bodies

The composition of governing bodies varies widely (Field, 1989); most are made up of people with widely differing interests in, and varying experiences of, current educational practice. The headteacher and teacher governor stand at one end of the spectrum and would generally be well acquainted with developments in special needs education since 1978; at the other end of the spectrum may be a very recently co-opted governor who has local business interests, maybe childless, and with experience limited to her own perhaps distant education. In the middle come the parent governors, usually with considerable interest in and varying levels of awareness of, current issues in special needs. In addition to this diversity within any one governing body, are the differences between the governing bodies of a large comprehensive school, a small rural primary school, and a special school. Because the governors of special schools would be much more aware of, and concerned with special needs issues, these remarks refer to governors in mainstream education, who for the most part have had no training in the field of special needs education.

What governing bodies do have in common in the consideration of children with special needs, are as follows: Firstly, they have certain statutory duties and responsibilities. Secondly, their powers have been increased by local management of resourcing, (Local Management of Schools — the administration of most of their own school's spending). Thirdly, and as a result of these powers, they must be aware of how budget allocation might affect the treatment of special educational need in their own school. What will the effects be on the integration of children into mainstream education? And in all of these areas governors are accountable to the parents.

Parental Influence and Involvement,

In the light of this accountability to parents it seems important to look briefly at the way parental influence has increased in the field of education before considering the statutory duties of the governors. Without this growth many of the Acts of the 1980s would not make sense. The government has tried to make the educator of the child more answerable to the parent, and at the same time to give the parent more influence in certain areas. Educational research has pointed to the importance of parental involvement, much of which has been in the field of reading (Hewison and Tizard, 1980; Bushell et.al. 1982; Tizard et al. 1982). Of particular interest is the study by Sigston et.al. (1984) indicating that those children with the greatest initial difficulties appeared to benefit the most. Partly as a result of this research reading schemes involving parents, and such facilities as toy libraries and family rooms, have grown up. The parents are encouraged to visit the school. In short, the general growth in parental participation and the belief that parents should participate has affected the child with special educational needs.

> Any system which excludes most parents but summons those whose children are having problems could be negative and counter-productive. (Pearson and Lindsay, 1986, p.70).

This research has been reflected by the growth of parents' organisations at local and national level, showing a concerned and articulate body. Parents are no longer willing to limit the PTA to good works; many PTAs discuss educational issues. Since the Plowden Report (1967), a Committee which recommended much greater parental participation in primary education and that parents should where possible send their child to the school of their choice, policies of parental involvement have gradually found their way into national legislation (see below). The government appears to wish to remove power from the hands of local authorities; this has resulted in greater central power, for setting up of *opting out* possibilities; it has also concentrated more power in the hands of the governing bodies of schools (for example, in the administration of the school's budget) and, since parents are represented on the governing bodies of schools, and governing bodies are now statutorily more accountable to parents, a growth of parental power and influence has been the result.

The statutory responsibilities of the governing body

The 1981 Education Act was an important one for children with special needs. It promoted integration of those children into mainstream schools, so long as it was compatible with the efficient education of all pupils and with the efficient use of resources. It involves parents at every stage and emphasises that children should be educated in accordance with their parents wishes. Circulars 1/83 and 22/89 re-emphasised the parental involvement. It is important to look at the other statutory responsibilities of the governing body bearing this Act in mind. In particular, under the 1981 Act, governors must use their best endeavours to provide for the children with special educational needs.

The National Curriculum and the child with special needs

The Education Act (1986) required that the governors study the LEA statement of curricular policy and decide in the light of this what the school's policy should be; this must take the form of a written and accessible statement. Since then the introduction of a National Curriculum means far less diversity in the curriculum is possible, but the governors still have the responsibility of *overseeing* the delivery of the National Curriculum, and must have a policy with regard to sex education. It is the governor's duty, with the headteacher and LEA, to 'secure' the provision of the National Curriculum. Before going on to consider this in relation to special educational needs it is worth quoting the Education Reform Act 1988 (1-25); the curriculum is all activities which promote the 'spiritual, moral, cultural, mental and physical development of pupils and which prepare pupils for the 'opportunities, responsibilities, and experiences of adult life'.

With the National Curriculum goes assessment at key stages and it has been said that the process of assessment will be one more experience of failure for these children. For statemented children and most of those in special schools the National Curriculum may be modified or disapplied. Perhaps, as has been suggested, the applications for statementing will increase. But the Warnock Report (DES 1978) has argued that 20 percent of children in mainstream education experience difficulty at some stage, and a smaller percentage experience persistent difficulty 'a significantly greater difficulty' in learning than the majority of children of that age. Governors must be aware of the sensitivity with which assessment of these non-statemented children must be carried out. Will there be many exemptions? Again, governors have a role here. For non-statemented children the head may decide that in some cases part or all of the National Curriculum may be temporarily disapplied. This period of time may not be more than 6 months and the head is required to inform the parents and the governors of this decision, its effect, and the provision made for the pupil during this time. They must also be told how the pupil is to be brought back into the National Curriculum unless it is proposed that the pupil be assessed because s/he has

50

special educational needs. Parents can appeal to the governing body over such a *disapplication*, or, if they wish the head to make such a temporary exemption and this is refused they can again appeal to the governing body. It is well worth reading the Appeals section of the Ace Handbook on the 1981 Act (Newell. 1988 3rd revised edition). Exemptions are dealt with in the DES Circular 15/89 and section 17 of the 1988 Education Act. When I discussed such exclusions with the Centre for Studies on Integration in Education, a spokesperson said she would hope that governors would try to ensure that such exemptions were as few as possible. The National Curriculum Council makes this point as well and all Governors should read its case on pupils with special educational needs:

> 'All pupils share the right to a broad and balanced curriculum, including the National Curriculum. The right extends to every pupil whether or not he or she has a statement of special educational needs. This right is implicit in the 1988 Educational Reform Act' (National Curriculum Council (2) 1989 p.1).

The argument is that the Curriculum is applicable to nearly all children, and the NCC goes on to give examples of different targets and levels for children with difficulties. It reiterates that exceptional arrangements should be kept to a minimum.

It certainly appears to be flying in the face of the governors' duty to bring about integration if there is a rush to exempt pupils, statemented or non-statemented, from the National Curriculum. However, there is no getting round the fact that the statutory assessment will underline the difference in the levels the pupil with learning difficulties will achieve and those expected to be achieved by most of their age group. The task group which worked on assessment did recommend most forcibly that each assessment be a positive and learning experience: 'Like all children, those with special educational needs require attainable targets to encourage their development and promote their self-esteem' (Task Group on Assessment and Testing, 1988 p.24).

Whatever the truth of this statement there is no doubt that assessment is a fact of current educational life: it should therefore be used positively. After such assessment it should be possible to detail exactly what sort of programme is needed for the child at that stage. Governors, whilst making sure that as many children as possible share the National Curriculum, must also remember their duties under the 1981 Education Act; that governors must use their *best endeavour* to provide what is needed for the pupil with special educational needs. This may often mean additional resourcing for support staff, special materials and, of course, aids for those with physical and sensory disabilities. Whereas previously the governor could lobby the LEA for extra resourcing, Local Management of Schools means that most of the resourcing is now in the hands of the governors. Governors will, in a sense, be lobbying their own governing bodies and determining resourcing priorities themselves.

LMS and the Role of the Governing Body

One of the greatest changes of the Education Act (1988) has been to transfer the larger part of the school's budget into the hands of the governors. The financial transfer of power started in a small way in 1986, when LEAs were required to furnish governors with an annual statement of the school's expenditure, and to make available to governors an annual sum for books, equipment, and stationery (section 29 (1) (a)). The 1988 Act followed with LMS, or Local Management of Schools, a facility now to be extended to all schools. All secondary schools and primary schools with over 200 on roll were to have the responsibility of administering their own budgets. The LEA was to delegate most of its spending power to boards of governors. there were items which had to be delegated (the day-to-day running and staffing of the school and purchase of stock), items which the LEA would retain (such as home-school transport, capital expenditure, and advisory services) and discretionary items which might be delegated or not, subject to a stringent limit on the proportion of the total which the LEA could retain. (Education Reform Act 1988, Sections 33-43, 48-51, Staffing Sections 44, 46-47, and Schedule 3). In theory this gives the governing body considerable power. It may determine where in the school to allocate resources, and where to remove them.

The bulk of spending is, of course, on staffing, where traditionally the governors have had the power of making appointments. Although this has been a role of the governing body for many years it has not before been combined with responsibility of resourcing such appointments. In the area of special needs it can easily be seen how much cheaper support staff such as ancillaries or welfare assistants are than a teacher trained in special needs and how expensive it is to employ one specialist for groups of 3 to 10 children. The following example illustrates what may happen.

In one primary school the classes were becoming larger and the special needs teacher who had groups of 4 to 8 children at a time withdrawn from the class was redeployed as a class teacher. With this extra teacher all the classes were made smaller and each teacher in that school became responsible for the identification of the child who needed support. In theory with the smaller classes this should have been easier. In fact, the only thing that we know for certain has been accomplished is a reduction in the size of the classes in that school. As one parent governor in the school pointed out, the school has lost that person whose specific job it was to identify and work on the delivery of a suitable curriculum for every child who needed support. The reply to this was that if each class teacher was totally responsible for the child with special educational needs then the process of integration would be accelerated — no more withdrawal. It could also be argued that to use the special needs teacher as a class teacher is 'compatible with the efficient use of resources'. It can be seen from this case study how very complicated staffing resources decisions will be. Governors have a duty to encourage the process of integration, but it is easy to see how expediency can work both for integration and against it and how integration might mean less support. Will there be a great increase in statemented children in mainstream schools because they bring more resources with them and would this be for or against the spirit of integration? The National Union of Teachers said of LMS and governors' powers,

> Often meeting only once a term, they are to be given but the briefest of training therefore embarking on much wider and substantial financial responsibilities which will affect each school in its daily life (NUT, 1988).

It is pleasant to imagine that all decisions will be well- informed and result in the best possible education for the greatest number of children, but it is true that allocation of resources may hinge on there being a well-informed and interested governor who is prepared to lobby his own governing body for the child with special needs.

In addition to these dilemmas of resource allocation, it should be remembered that schools may not be better off. It has been pointed out that for every school which is a winner with formula funding, i.e. has more money than previously, there should also be a loser, a school which is worse off. It has already become apparent that primary schools are to be catered for less generously than secondary schools. However, secondary schools with falling rolls are also faced with the loss of several staff. Such losses, depending on where the cuts are made, may have a drastic effect on support for the pupil with learning difficulties.

The implications of local resourcing of schools are far-reaching and it is impossible to say whether there will be a sharp increase in statementing to extract more money for the school with the statemented child. In general, statementing is a slow process and this would not be a quick route to additional funding. It is difficult to foresee how governing bodies will cope with the budgeting in view of the diversity of such bodies. It remains to be seen how much the LEA will reduce service for special needs. The LEA will still be responsible for centrally run services such as the educational psychologists, Section XI grants, and specialist services like the support team for special needs staff. For example, there has been much debate recently in Oxfordshire about the cutting of the Special Needs Advisory and Support Teachers. Such teams were based in different areas of the county and did invaluable work in supporting teachers concerned with special educational needs. They visit schools, suggest materials and curriculum adaptations, carry successful schemes from one school to another, keep special needs teachers in touch with work elsewhere, and work to involve the parents in reading schemes. However, the reduction of money available to the LEA for such county funded schemes is likely to mean severe reductions in these services, from which the child with difficulties had benefited.

Conclusion

It is impossible to draw conclusions at the start of a period which will see such an expansion of the governor's role in relation to special educational needs. A year ago I questioned a number of primary school governors about their attitudes to special needs in their schools. In general they felt that every help should be given to such children, but only one governor had actually thought of the possible impact of LMS. The gulf between the knowledge of the head and teacher governors and the rest of the governors was enormous, as one might expect, but one or two governors admitted they had never really thought much about the child with special needs. On the other hand a school in the same area which had the reputation for a less formal and more progressive regime had governors who showed considerable interest in the whole question. How many primary schools do have a policy document on Special Needs?

In contrast to this I have spoken to several governors of medium to large comprehensives; they seemed better informed, more interested and anxious to protect services for children with special needs, and either had, or were in the process of setting up, working parties to look at the issues of integration and increased support in the classroom. Several governors had voiced disquiet at the poor training given to support staff, and the lack of career structure or incentive in this low paid work. They were delighted with the news that support staff were to be included in INSET days in their county and felt governors should be aware of the quality, and quantity of support offered in their own school. This anxiety over the level of support was also voiced by the Centre for Studies in Integration in Education where a spokeswoman pointed out that integration without proper support services to meet the needs of that child was not integration at all, but dumping. The same theme is echoed in Hahoney (1988) where he talks of *pseudo-assimilation* of the child with special educational needs or *disintegration* in mainstream schools.

It is worth quoting a Scottish parent who had just fought successfully to remove her child from an integrated unit at a primary school to a special independently run school 'I have no doubt that for the primary children it was a learning experience to have Graham with them, but I seriously doubt that he gained anything from it'. She wanted him to learn social skills such as feeding himself and the school wanted to teach him to write (The Scotsman, 24th January 1990, p.19). These are precisely the issues governors must be aware of. They should constantly question what the system is offering the child. One interested and well-informed governor of the same school wanted to know what other countries did. How had integration worked elsewhere? What lessons could be learned from comparative studies? How do other countries deal with what many teachers find the most difficult challenge to face — the pupil with behavioural problems? Too often the argument for integration concentrates on the child with physical and sensory disabilities, and yet many teachers find those with the short concentration span, learning difficulties and behaviour problems far more of a challenge to integrate successfully. It is part of the governors' role to stand back and form links with other schools, to be aware of practices in other counties, and to be interested in what happens in other countries.

What it is possible to say is that most governors genuinely concerned with the pupils at that school would welcome additional training. LEAs at present are offering various training packages but special needs does not figure large in most of them. The BBC (1998) is one package which does go into special needs in its curriculum concerns, and it is to be hoped that each governing body will either name one person whose responsibility it is for special needs or, better still, assume that it is the responsibility of every governor. Joan Sallis (1988) suggests that regular reports be made to the governors by the staff of the school who are concerned with special needs. The Centre for Studies on Integration in Education produce a mine of relevant information on integration and all governors should be aware of the lack of real progress in the integration of children with special needs into mainstream education (Swann, 1989). How many schools have any links with special schools, as the Warnock Report recommended.

I am aware that governors who read this may well experience a sinking feeling. Here is another set of responsibilities in what is a voluntary commitment. Most governors have many other demands on their time. The comment I heard from one governor must be fairly typical of many governors' feelings 'What's happened to the Christmas sherry and the termly discussion of the state of the boys' loos?' This was the complaint of one long serving governor as she resigned last year. Whatever individual governors feel about their increased work load and role in special needs, there is little doubt that the vast majority of governors support increased parental involvement. If parents have not had the experience of their own child's difficulty at some time they almost certainly know other parents who have. So long as the parental influence is strong in the governing body, and parents of those children with special needs are aware of their rights and involvement with every stage of education, then it seems likely that governing bodies will become more aware of their responsibilities to the children who have special educational needs. Those children and young people most vulnerable in competition for limited resources and attention are surely those with special educational needs. The governor has a duty to attend to these needs.

Acknowledgements

I am grateful to the Governors of Oxfordshire schools who gave their valuable time to talk to me.

References

ACE Bulletin No 32. (1989) *Exceptions To The Rule,* Nov-Dec 1989, London: ACE.

BBC Education (1989) Curriculum Concerns, Audio cassette produced by Villiers, J. London.

Bussell, R., Miller, A., and Robson, D. (1982) 'Parents as remedial teachers', *Assoc. of Educational Psychologists Journal,* 5,9, pp.7-13.

CSIE, (1989) *Integration and Resources,* The Centre for Studies on Integration in Education: London.

Department of Education and Science (1978) Special Educational Needs (Warnock Report). London: HMSO.

Department of Education and Science (1988a) Report of the Task Group on Assessment and Testing, London, DES and Welsh Office.

Department of Education and Science, (1989b) 'School Governors: A Guide to the Law: county and controlled schools'. London, DES.

Department of Education and Science, (1989a) Education Reform Act 1988, Circular 15/89: Temporary Exceptions from the National Curriculum, London, DES.

Department of Education and Science, (1989b) Circular 22/89 Assessments and Statements of Special Educational Needs: Procedures within the Education, Health and Social Services, London: DES.

Field, L. (1989) 'School governing bodies'. *Curriculum,* Autumn 1988, Vol.10, No.2, pp.108-112.

Henderson, M. (1990) 'Suitable Cases for Special Treatment' *The Scotsman,* 24th January. 1990, p.19.

Hewison, J. and Tizard, J. (1980) 'Parental involvement and reading assessment', Brit. of Educational Psychology, 50, pp.209-215.

Mahoney, T. (1988) *Governing Schools: Powers, Issues and Practice,* Macmillan Education Hampshire and London.

National Union of Teachers (1988) *Financing Schools: the Response of the National Union of Teachers to the Government's proposals.* NUT: London.

Newell, P. (1988) ACE Special Education Handbook, Third Revised Edition, London.

Plowden Report (1967) *Children and their Primary Schools.* HMSO: London.

Pearson, L. and Lindsay, G. (1986) *Special Needs in the Primary School: Identification and Intervention,'* NFER-Nelson: Windsor.

Robbins, B. (1989) 'There's a place for us', *Junior Education,* Oct. 1989 pp.35.

Sallis, J. (1988) *Schools, Parents and Governors: A New Approach to Accountability.* Routledge: London.

Sigston, A., Addington, L., Banks, V., and Striesow, M. (1984) 'Progress with Parents: an account and evaluation of a home reading project for poor readers' *Remedial Education,* 19, pp.170-173.

Swann, W. (1989) *Integration Statistics — LEAs Reveal Local Variations.* The Centre for Studies on Integration in Education: London.

Tizard, J., Schofield, W.N. and Hewison, J. (1982) 'Collaboration between teachers and parents in assisting children's reading', *Brit. Jnl. of Educational Psychology.* 52, pp.1-15.

Vaughan, M. (1989) Parents, Children and the Legal Framework, in Roaf, C., and Bines, H. (Eds.) (1989) *Needs, Rights and Opportunities: Developing Approaches to Special Education,* Lewes: Falmer Press.

Part 2

Aspects of the Curriculum and assessment

Chapter 5

Mathematics and Pupils with Special Needs

Hilary Shuard

Pupils with special needs in mathematics

Pupils who have special educational needs in mathematics suffer from a variety of disabilities and difficulties. Some children have physical, emotional or behavioural disabilities, while others find mathematics exceptionally easy or exceptionally difficult: some have a combination of difficulties. Some children have special needs in mathematics throughout their schooldays, while others have them for only a comparatively short time. The Warnock Report (DES, 1978) estimated that about one child in five would have special educational needs at some time during their schooldays, and about one child in six might have these needs at any particular time. An HMI report in 1990 (DES, 1990) supported this estimate, and pointed out that the vast majority (over 90%) of children with special educational needs are educated in ordinary schools. Thus, ordinary schools contain very large numbers of pupils who have special needs in mathematics.

This chapter will concentrate on one group of children with special needs, those in primary and secondary schools who are very low attainers in mathematics compared with their peers. We will discuss first the arrangements for teaching them, then their mathematical needs, and finally the impact of the National Curriculum.

The Warnock Committee estimated that children with learning difficulties were the largest group of those with special needs:

> We see these children [with mild learning difficulties] as forming the largest proportion at all those who, in our view, require special educational provision. (DES, 1978, para. 11.49)

Several studies in the last ten years or so have shown that the range of attainment in mathematics among children of the same age is very great. The Cockcroft Report (DES, 1982) on the teaching of mathematics in primary and secondary schools called this wide range of attainment the 'seven year difference'. After studying evidence from large-scale testing of mathematical attainment in the work of the Assessment of Performance Unit (APU) in England and Wales, and similar evidence from Scotland, the USA and Australia, it concluded that:

> There is a 'seven year difference' in achieving an understanding of place value which is sufficient to write down the number which is 1 more that 6399. By this we mean that, whereas an 'average' child can perform this task at age 11 but not at age 10, there are some 14 year olds who cannot do it and some 7 year olds who can. Similarly comparisons can be made in respect of other topics. (DES, 1982, para.342)

The APU surveyed large samples of children at the age of 11 and 15. As a result of this testing they divided the children into five attainment bands, each comprising 20% of the children surveyed. They found that in many of the tasks surveyed the performance of the lowest 20% at age 15 was comparable with that of the next 20% at age 11 (APU 1985). Some examples are given in the table overleaf: the five attainment bands are labelled B (bottom), LM (lower middle), M (middle), UM (upper middle), T (top).

In this table, the facility of an item is the percentage of children of a particular age who get it right. It can be seen that the success rate of the bottom attainment band at age 15 is very similar to that of the lower middle attainment band at age 11. In other words, the lowest attaining 20% of children have progressed very slowly in their ability to perform these tasks during nearly five years in the secondary school.

Pencil and paper tasks such as these form a convenient measure of pupils' attainment in mathematics. However, they form only a very small sample of the range of ways in which mathematics is used. Writing down the number which is 1 more than 399 is a very different type of task from paying for something costing £3.99 by giving £4 and expecting to receive 1p. change. The second task is based on real experience with coins, while the first demands that the child should generalise from this and other concrete experiences to form an abstract idea about numbers. Pupils' ability to use mathematics in real-life ways may be very different from their ability to perform a pencil and paper task; too much reliance should not be placed on the results of pencil and paper tests of limited ranges of skills and concepts.

Table 1: Facilities of some mathematical tasks, by 20% attainment bands

Item	Age	Attainment band				
		B	LM	M	UM	T
The number which is one less than 2010 is...	11	18	64	87	94	98
	15	57	88	94	97	100
Write $\frac{4}{100}$ as a decimal	11	2	9	28	55	88
Write $\frac{3}{100}$ as a decimal	15	4	25	56	80	97
Comparing angles	11	26	36	52	67	89
	15	33	62	89	97	100

(Based on APU, 1985)

Low attainment in mathematics may arise from physical, mental or emotional causes within the pupil, which the child and the school have to continue to live with, or from causes within his or her home circumstances. Low attainment may also arise from causes within the school, over which the school may have some control. Larcombe (1988) gives a list of circumstances within the school which he believed may contribute to low attainment in mathematics. They are:

Lesson length and timetable unsuitable.
Group size too large.
Mathematics room drab and uninspiring.
All teaching by exposition to the whole class.
No specialist support teaching available, though needed.
Teaching style and content unsuited to pupil needs.
Teacher has little confidence in mathematics.
No practical apparatus available.
Only unsuitable published materials available.

Although some items in this apply more obviously to secondary schools than to primary schools, others are equally applicable to both phases. All schools need to look carefully at their own practice, to determine whether any of the reasons for children having special needs in mathematics might be grounded in the mathematics teaching that pupils have received in the school, rather than in external causes. It is possible that some improvement may be made through changes in the school's own practice, and that changes in the school's practice might also diminish the number of pupils with special needs in mathematics in the future.

Arrangement for teaching mathematics to children with special needs

In their recent report of education provision for children with special needs (DES, 1990), HMI warned:

> This sector is not well prepared to meet the challenges of the 1990s, such as those of the National Curriculum and local management of schools. (DES, 1990)

This conclusion was largely based on an HMI survey of children with special needs in ordinary schools, which was carried out in 1988-9 (HMI 1989). In this survey, pupils in the age-groups 10-11 and 11-12 were tracked by HMI for the whole of a school day. The Inspectors therefore observed a good deal of mathematics with these pupils, in addition to other curriculum areas. In about half the lessons observed in both primary and secondary schools (in all subjects) the quality of the work seen was considered to be 'satisfactory or better'. However, HMI made the following comment on mathematics lessons which they judged to be of unsatisfactory quality:

> In mathematics, work of unsatisfactory quality was frequently associated with pupils being given large numbers of computation exercises, which some pupils completed incorrectly since they were given no objects which they could use to count and cluster as a means of helping them to understand the number of relationships involved. HMI, 1989)

HMI did see some very good mathematics lessons, and thought that an essential factor in excellence was the 'careful matching of learning tasks to pupils' differing achievements'. One description of excellent mathematics was of a lesson with a mixed ability secondary class, in which all the pupils worked on the same topic at a range of tasks which were suitably matched to each pupil.

A major theme in the HMIs' perception of the quality of work was the importance of differentiating the work according to the needs of individuals. This is of particular importance in mathematics, where the range of attainment is so great, and where pupils are often given closed tasks at which they either fail or succeed, with little opportunity allowed for different interpretations of success. HMI summed up as follows:

> In almost half the primary school lessons seen differentiation was not satisfactory. In the secondary schools, as in the primary schools, poor differentiation of the learning tasks was a major contributory factor to work of unsatisfactory quality, and was an issue yet be addressed satisfactorily in half the classes visited.

HMI also commented about the good-quality work that they saw:

> Work of at least satisfactory quality was often associated with experi-
> ence-based learning activities which used a range of media and prac-
> tical tasks. (HMI, 1989)

HMI noted that in some schools, in both primary and secondary phases,
pupils with special needs worked for the whole week alongside their peers
in mainstream classes, while in other school they were extracted for part of
the week to work in smaller groups, often on basic skills in language and
mathematics. In some schools, pupils with special needs received additional
support teaching within their own classroom, the support teacher working
alongside the class teacher. These methods of organisation meant that some
pupils with special needs were taught mathematics by more than one teacher,
and extraction from the class might mean that they were only present for
some of the mathematics lessons each week in their own class. When pupils
were extracted from their own class for some of the mathematics lessons
each week, very careful planning was needed to ensure that these pupils
received continuity of learning in mathematics; it was clear, however, that
this planning only sometimes took place.

Some pupils with special needs were not receiving a broad and balanced
curriculum. For example, in some secondary schools bottom sets receive a
separate, and limited, curriculum:

> For one-third of all the secondary pupils seen their curriculum lacked
> this essential breadth. This was [often due] to a system which grouped
> these pupils in bottom sets which were offered a separate curriculum,
> much of which concentrated on teaching a restricted diet of narrowly
> conceived language and computational skills.

The most alarming thing about this HMI survey is its very recent date. A
more detailed, but older, description of the difficulties suffered by some
pupils with special needs is given in Hart *et.al.* (1989). This is an account of
a research project on *Children's Mathematical Frameworks* undertaken in
1983-5.

Teachers were asked to teach a series of mathematics lessons in which
children were introduced to a mathematical idea, which was then formalised
into a procedure that the children would be expected to retain and use. Six
children from each class were interviewed three times during the series of
lessons and once three months after the end of the lessons; some lessons
were also observed by the researchers. All the teachers were experienced
practitioners who volunteered to take part in the research.

One series of lessons was with a small remedial class of nine twelve-year-
olds in a middle school. They were taught the standard procedure for
subtraction with decomposition: the design of the lessons included a great
deal of experience of practical subtraction using base ten blocks. For all the
children, this was not the first time they had attempted to learn this procedure.

Decomposition is based on the fact that a number can be rearranged (or decomposed) without its value being changed: for example, to carry out 63-27, 6 tens and 3 units are decomposed into 5 tens and 13 units. Three months after the end of the series of lessons, four of the six children interviewed thought that decomposition did change the value of the number decomposed. More fundamentally, decomposition is based on an under-standing of place value. To enquire into this, the children were asked, at interview, how many bags of 10 sweets could be made up from 367 sweets. Only three of the six children could answer this question in a satisfactory way.

The teacher of this class also took it for granted that the children would use number bonds that they knew in the subtraction. Unfortunately, this was not the case; all the children counted on their fingers or needed apparatus for a calculation such as 17-9. Thus, 2-digit or 3-digit subtraction was a much more laborious process for them than the teacher realised.

This series of lessons was not in fact well matched to the children's actual understanding of number although the teacher was correct in believing that the children did not understand the process of decomposition. Unfortunately, they continued not to understand it after a great deal of hard work.

The mathematical needs of children with special educational needs

Why should children with special needs learn mathematics?
The first and over-riding reason that all children, including those with special needs should learn some mathematics is that it is useful to them. This reason is more complex than it may seem at first.

Mathematics is useful in pupils' lives outside school, both at present and as they look to the future, when they will take on adult responsibilities. Many forms of employment also require some mathematical knowledge and skills. The most obviously useful areas of mathematical content are *money* and *time*. Even the simplest forms of daily living make some use of these, and of the ability to *count*. However, mathematical content is not the only aspect of mathematics that is useful. Denvir, Stolz and Brown (1982), in a study of *Low Attainers in Mathematics: 5-16,* have pointed out that:

> Most jobs, at the least, require employees to plan logically and follow ordered procedures as, for example, in fault-finding and turning-on procedures for machinery.

These mathematical processes of logical thinking and planning are as important a part of mathematics as the content of topics such as number.

Mathematics can also help people to lead a fuller life, enabling them to carry out tasks such as playing games that require scoring, planning the sensible spending of income, and planning trips and holidays.

In school, other subject areas make use of mathematics, and pupils need some mathematical understanding in order to progress in other subjects. However, the necessary links are not always made. In one HMI survey of secondary schools, HMI asked themselves three specific questions about links between mathematics and other subjects:

Is the teaching positively related to the calculations required in science?

Is the teaching positively related to the calculations required in crafts?

Is the teaching positively related to the use of mathematics in other subject areas?

(DES 1979)

In respect of 'non-examination' courses (below O-level and CSE) for fourth- and fifth-year secondary pupils, HMI answered 'no' to all three questions of over 85% of cases. This survey was carried out in the late 1970s; it is to be hoped that there has been a great improvement, so that pupils do not continue to find themselves handicapped in the rest of their schooling by mathematical difficulties.

The Cockcroft Report (DES, 1982) saw the most powerful reason for teaching mathematics to be its power as a means of communication:

In our view the mathematics teacher has the task... above all, of making each pupil aware that mathematics provides him with a powerful means of communication. (DES, 1982, para.12)

Thus, the Cockcroft Committee saw mathematics as a form of language. A major task in the education of children with special needs is to develop their language and their powers of communication: mathematics should not be omitted from this task.

In addition to being useful and an important means of communication, mathematics is found by some people to be interesting in itself — an activity which gives them pleasure. Denvir, Stolz and Brown ask us:

If a valid component of the education of the more successful pupil should be the pleasure of discovering the solutions to problems and in aesthetically appreciating patterns in number and form, should not this be equally true for the less successful pupil even though the pleasure may result from work at a simple level? (Denvir, Stolz and Brown, 1982)

Among the examples these authors provide is an instance in which four low-attaining six-year-olds were playing Beetle, with the support of a card from which they traced the outline of the Beetle and a coding card listing '6 for a body', '5 for a head' etc. They had to recognise the numeral in order to trace the appropriate part of the Beetle:

> They enjoyed explaining to the project team member how to play and watched each other carefully to make sure no mistakes were made. (Denvir, Stolz and Brown, 1982)

Needs in the classroom

The classroom needs of pupils with special needs in mathematics are not different from the needs of other children. As HMI remarked in their recent survey of special needs:

> The main features of practice which resulted in work of at least satisfactory standard among pupils with special educational needs also constituted good practice for all pupils. (HMI 1989)

However, many pupils with special needs have experienced even more vivid episodes of failure in mathematics than their higher attaining peers. Many pupils, whatever their level of attainment, think that mathematics is a difficult subject. In the APU's surveys of pupils' attitudes to mathematics (APU, 1985), over 30% of pupils said that mathematics was difficult to some degree, and there was some correlation between their opinions of the difficulty of mathematics and their performance in the written mathematics tests. Girls thought that mathematics was significantly more difficult than did boys.

By the time that they come to the end of the compulsory school years, many children dislike mathematics, and, as the APU found:

> Girls' scores for enjoyment are consistently lower than those of boys. (APU, 1985)

Thus, among low attainers in mathematics there is a sizeable group of pupils who experience regular failure in mathematics, find it difficult, and dislike it. A majority of the children with poor attitudes to mathematics are girls, although there may be more boys than girls among low attainers in mathematics.

A report by Haylock (1986) describes a project in which questionnaires about possible characteristics of low attainers in mathematics were sent to a group of middle school teachers. The teachers were asked to indicate, for each low attaining 9-10 year old in their class (these children were identified by a NFER mathematics test), how far each of a variety of possible descriptions applied to that child. Descriptions were obtained of 215 children, 126 boys and 89 girls. Haylock found that:

> It is very commonly the case that the low attainer in mathematics will have been considered a low attainer for some time, will be low

attaining in most areas of the curriculum and in all aspects of mathematics, and will have poor reading and language skills.

More often for low attaining boys that for girls is it the case that the child shows little commitment and interest in school in general, displays behaviour problems, appears preoccupied, finding school and learning irrelevant, and behaves particularly badly in front of other children. On the other hand the low attaining girls show significantly higher levels of anxiety towards mathematics. (Haylock 1986)

It seems clear from these studies that among the classroom needs of pupils with special needs in mathematics, an aim which must rank very high is for the teacher to win their interest and co- operation, to alleviate anxiety, and to help them to avoid failure. The same is also true for higher-attaining pupils, many of who have similar feelings of difficulty and dislike.

Not all children learn in the same way, and, in order to give maximum opportunity for learning, they need to experience a variety of teaching styles in the mathematics classroom. The Cockcroft Report (DES, 1982) stressed the importance of six styles of teaching:

Mathematics teaching at all levels should include opportunities for

- exposition by the teacher;
- discussion between teacher and pupils and between pupils themselves;
- appropriate practical work;
- consolidation and practice of fundamental skills and routines;
- problem solving, including the application of mathematics to everyday situations;
- investigational work.

(DES, 1982, para. 243)

Not all teachers, at any level, provide experiences of all these types of learning for their pupils; indeed, some teachers seem to believe that pupils with special needs are not capable of problem-solving or investigational work. However, a group of teachers working with the PrIME (Primary Initiatives in Mathematical Education) project wrote an interesting account of simple investigations and the use of pattern with low-attaining children aged between six and eleven years (Shuard et.al, 1990). Among the activities used were exploring the variety of models that could be made with five multilink cubes, making larger and larger triangles by putting circular counters together, different ways of making ten with multilink, and exploring the range of possible ten-spot dominoes that could be made. The children also explored number tracks and numbers grids, looking for patterns and piecing together jigsaws made from number grids. In all these activities the thinking was simple, but it was the children's own. The group concluded its descriptions of the last activity as follows:

> The children enjoyed the activities, but they found the 'worms' [strips cut from number grids] so difficult that the teacher completely re-thought their subsequent activities. She realised that to get through her planned task, she had substituted teacher over-involvement and rote procedures for mathematical thinking by the children... The group are now making good progress, and when they returned to grid work with the 100 square, many of the patterns they had brushed against earlier were readily recalled. In fact, the value of activity-based work and investigational work may not be clear at once. (Shauard *et.al, 1990, activity F6*)

Haylock (1987) emphasises the importance of developing links between language and children's mathematical activity. He describes the following incident as an illustration of a way in which activity, language and symboli-sation were linked together. A group of low-attaining ten year olds were having difficulty with early stages of learning about division. They shared 12 pennies between 3 people, used *Breakthrough to Literacy* cards to make up sentences such as, 12 shared between 3 is 4 each' and '3 sets of 4 make 12 altogether', and drew the 3 sets of 4. The next step was to try to connect the experience and the language with the mathematical symbolisms $4 \times 3 = 12$ and $12 \div 3 = 4$. Here the calculator had a useful role; the children checked their results on the calculator, and by recording the keys they pressed, achieved the statements $4 \times 3 = 12$ and $12 \div 3 = 4$.

Many pupils with special needs in mathematics also find difficulty in reading. A common style of teaching in mathematics makes much use of written material in the form of textbooks, workcards and worksheets. Jones (1976) studies the ability of 9- 10 year old children in third-year junior classes in Sheffield to read the mathematics textbooks which they used in class. All the (commonly used) books investigated had a reading age of 12 or higher, and two-thirds or more of the children had a reading age below that of the textbook they were using. This group no doubt contained all the children with special needs in mathematics, whose mathematical difficulties must be compounded by reading difficulties. Haylock recommends:

> The first step in trying to help such pupils must be to throw out the commercially published scheme... For those for whom reading pro-duces excessive strain the printed word is always going to be the least successful way of trying to teach them.

Nor is the commonly used device of producing workcards which make a minimal use of words, and rely on using mathematical symbols, likely to be successful. The task of reading symbols with understanding is itself difficult, as an unknown symbol among a set of symbols usually provides fewer cues to its meaning than does an unknown word in a passage of text (Shuard and Rothery 1984).

If pupils are to develop their oral language in mathematics, they need to work together, so that discussion can take place, and sharing can enable them to support one another. A teacher in a school for children with moderate learning difficulties described his year's work in mathematics in the journal *Struggle* (Lewis, 1989). Among the points he made were:

[In working with the computer program 'L'] we had some excellent sessions which were enjoyable and highly educational. There was a considerable amount of co-operative work.

It does not matter who does the teaching. If a pupil can learn a good method or procedure from another pupil it is just as worthwhile as if they learnt it from me.

Work does not need to be rigidly at the right level. (Lewis, 1989)

Some of Lewis's pupils surprised him very much with what they were able to do when they saw the activities as relevant, and wanted to do them for their own reasons. He would not have provided activities which made such demands if the pupils had not led the way.

New technology in the mathematics curriculum for pupils with special educational needs

In their everyday lives, very few people can avoid handling money and making simple calculations when shopping. Many adults seem to find it difficult to calculate with any but small numbers, as was shown by research undertaken for the Cockcroft Committee concerning the mathematical needs of adult life:

Many strategies were encountered for coping with the mathematical demands of everyday life. These included always buying £10 worth of petrol, always paying by cheque, always taking far more money than was likely to be needed... There was frequent reliance on husbands, wives or children to check and pay bills, to measure or to read timetables; and also reliance on past experience. (DES, 1982, para.30)

For all the people described in that passage, a calculator would be an extremely useful tool in their lives because it is cheap, easily portable in pocket or handbag, and gives not only quick results but also confidence. Many of the people interviewed for the Cockcroft research had access to a calculator, but either did not know how to use it or did not trust it to give correct and intelligible results.

A very important aim of mathematics teaching for pupils with special needs in mathematics must be to help them to be comfortable with calculators, so that they see the calculator as an important personal tool and build up their skill and confidence in using it. Indeed, for almost everyone, the most important piece of mathematical equipment for adult life is a calculator. People cannot go on, in adult life, using the specialised mathematical apparatus, such as multilink or base ten blocks, which they used at school. Important though that apparatus was when it was used, it needs to be replaced by something available and portable in adult life.

Calculators not only take the labour out of calculation but also release time in school to allow children to come to terms with other extremely importantly aspects of calculation which are often not treated as thoroughly as is needed. These aspects include: what each arithmetic operation means, which operations to use in particular situations, and how to apply the answer back to the situation. There is no value in being able to do a calculation if you cannot use that calculation to help to solve the daily problems of your own life.

Part of the work of the recent PrIME project mentioned earlier was to devise a Calculator-Aware Number (CAN) curriculum for children in primary schools (Shuard *et.al.,* 1991). The project team has worked with teachers to develop CAN in about twenty primary schools since 1986. The classes of these teachers have contained their share of children with special needs in mathematics, as does every class. It has become clear that a calculator does not at once transform a low-attaining child's understanding of mathematics because a calculator only helps with the actual calculation — it does not tell the child which key to press to solve a particular problem. However, a calculator may transform the confidence of a low-attaining child. 'I'm *good* at maths' said one very low-attaining CAN seven-year- old to the teacher, 'I wish I was as good at reading and writing as I am at maths'.

Using a calculator can do much more than merely assisting with calculations. It gives another way in which children can explore numbers for themselves, and find out how they work. It is impossible to stop children 'playing' with their calculators, and a calculator is the first 'toy' that embodies the number system, and that allows children to explore numbers as they 'play'. The CAN children have explored large numbers, negative numbers and decimals at a much earlier stage than would be expected in a conventional curriculum — and they have done this of their own initiative, not because the teacher insisted on it. Of course, the more able and confident children explore much further, but all undertake some exploration, and low-attaining children explore numbers at the level at which the exploration will help them.

The next incident gives an example of the way in which the demands of the calculator can change children's need for understanding of numbers. An advisory teacher interviewed a low- attaining CAN 8-year-old to explore her understanding of number operations. Part of the conversation, which was tape-recorded, went like this:

T: Take 9 from 30.

C: 21.

T: How did you do it?

C: I counted 30 in my mind and counted 9 down.

T: Can you tell me what 6 lots of 4 are?

C: 24.

T: How did you do it?

C: I kept on counting on 4 each time.

T: Could you do it on the calculator?
    [The child does 4 + 4 + 4 + 4 + 4 + 4 =]

T: Can you share 16 sweets between 3 people?

C: They will all get 5 and there will be one left over.

T: Do you ever use the calculator for sharing?
    [The child does 16 ÷ 3 and gets 5.3333333]

T: What does it mean?

C: I think it's wrong.

T: Let's do one in our heads first. 13 sweets shared by 2 people.

C: They both get 6 and there's one left over.

T: Try it on the calculator.
    [The child does 13 ÷ 2 and gets 6.5]

T: What is that showing?

C: 6 and a little bit.... That's how much they get. The .5 is the bit left over.

Children who use calculators cannot avoid meeting decimals. If they are not encouraged to make sense of decimals at school, they will join the ranks of those who would find a calculator very useful, but who mistrust the calculator because they do not understand what it is doing. The child in the last incident was only beginning to get to grips with decimals, at the age of eight. She will need much more experience of sharing things that can be cut up into fractions, sharing sums of money (such as sharing £13 between 2 people), talking about fractions and relating them to decimals on the calculator, and many other experiences, if she is to leave school as a confident calculator user.

In their recent report (DES, 1990), HMI referred to the importance of information technology (IT) in the education of pupils with SEN. It is clear, however, that they were referring only to computers, not to the importance of calculators as personal tools.

However, computers do also have an important part to play in the education of pupils with special needs in mathematics. HMI points out that:

> Information technology is less prevalent in primary schools, and pupils with special educational needs tend to have particularly limited access to it. In secondary schools, use with pupils with special educational needs tends to be by specialists in SEN only, principally for consolidating skills rather than for more creative activities, and there is little awareness among subject specialists of the possibilities of information technology for these pupils.

> The best practice in the support of pupils and students with special educational needs through information technology is associated with the use of a small number of powerful and flexible programmes.

In mathematics, these powerful and flexible programs include Logo, a database such as OURFACTS, adventure games and simulations such as MARTELLO TOWER and TEASHOP, investigational programs such as ERGO, and some rather more specialised programs such as COUNTER and TESSELLATIONS. An excellent list of good quality software resources is found in *New Technology in Primary Mathematics: INSET Resources* (MESU, 1989). Watchman (1990) gives an account of the use of DART (a simplified version of Logo) and Logo with pupils with special educational needs in a junior school. She concludes a description of work with two particular boys.

> By the time they finished in their third year in the school they had mastered concepts in mathematics and IT which are not normally requested of students until they are in the middle years of their secondary schooling... Turtling at the Ridge School is no longer the exclusive preserve of children with special educational needs. (Watchman, 1990)

The purpose of these powerful and flexible programs is to hand the control of the program over to the pupils, who are enabled to investigate and explore mathematical ideas through their own thinking rather than at the behest of the program. For example, the simplest uses of Logo are as a tool for drawing, either on the computer screen or with a 'floor Turtle'. A great deal of mathematics is used and learnt in instructing the program to draw, but the children make their own decisions about what to draw.

Problem solving and investigation for pupils with SEN in mathematics.

The important trends in mathematics teaching in the last few years, with pupils of all ages and abilities, have included the growth of *problem-solving* and *investigation,* and within problem-solving, the growing use of what have come to be called *'real problems'*.

The Cockcroft Report listed among its six recommended styles of teaching:

- Problem solving, including the application of mathematics to everyday situations.

- Investigational work.

(DES, 1982, para.243)

The Report went on to explain reasons for the importance of these:

> Mathematics is only 'useful' to the extent to which it can be applied to a particular situation and it is the ability to apply mathematics to a variety of situations to which we give the name 'problem-solving'... At each stage of the mathematics course the teacher needs to help pupils to understand how to apply the concepts and skills which are being learned and how to make use of them to solve problems. (DES, 1982, para.249)

> The idea of investigation is fundamental both to the study of mathematics itself and also to an understanding of the ways in which mathematics can be used to extend knowledge and to solve problems in very many fields. (DES, 1982, para.250)

For many pupils with special needs in mathematics, a major reason for learning mathematics is that it will be useful to them. It is one of the tools for tackling the problems of their everyday lives, not only at the present time, but also when they are adults. These pupils probably need more support from the school, as they learn to use mathematics as a problem-solving tool, than do their higher-attaining and more resourceful peers. Problem- solving in mathematics is thus an essential part of their education: within this, tackling 'real problems' is especially important.

'Real problems' occur in the daily life of every person and every school. Some of the school's problems, which use mathematics in their solution, may be:

> What food should be provided for the class picnic?
> How much will the school journey cost?
> How many pencils need to be ordered for next year?
> How should the seating for the Christmas concert be arranged?

When real problems occur in school, there is a strong temptation for teachers to solve them rather than to give opportunities for pupils to work on the problems for themselves in the same way that they will have to work on their own problems as adults. Thus, many of the uses of mathematics in the life of a school are hidden from pupils. Pupils also have mathematical problems of their own, such as:

How shall I spend my pocket money?
Can I afford...?
How can I get to... on time?
Does the new bus timetable make a difference to me?

Often, these problems are banished from the classroom, but examples of (almost) real problems at secondary level are to be found in the writings of the Spode Group, (undated), 198?). An interesting account of a primary class's investigation of school dinners is given in the PrIME materials (Shuard *et.al.*, 1990a). In response to a discussion started by pupils, the class investigated the different meals that could be bought from that day's menu by pupils who came with different amounts of dinner money.

If real problems are not admitted to the classroom, it should be no surprise if pupils think of mathematics as a subject which has little relevance to them. Other opportunities for problem-solving and investigation occur within mathematics itself. In a traditional style of mathematics teaching all mathematics is communicated to pupils by the teacher, and pupils then work exercises to practise what they have learnt. In a more exploratory style of teaching, pupils are often provided with problems and investigations, and are expected to use their knowledge and ingenuity to tackle these. Burton (1984) states some of the advantages of this method:

> The greatest value of this approach is in the effect it has on the classroom. Hesitancy and dependency in pupils are replaced by confidence and autonomy. Dislike of mathematics turns to enjoyment, indeed enthusiasm. Low self-images are replaced by expressions of authority. The change in pedagogical style gives teachers the opportunity, sometimes for the first time, to observe pupils and listen to their discussions. (Burton 1984, 9- 10)

Teachers who have not previously much used this method in mathematics can gain support from books such as *Problem solving in primary schools* (Fisher, 1987) and *Generating Mathematical Activity in the Classroom* (Bird, 1983). Bird describes how she encouraged a mixed-ability class of first-year secondary pupils to pose their own questions to investigate:

> I found that one particularly fruitful way of opening up a situation was to introduce a 'starter' to the whole class, invite the pupils to work at it for a short time, ask them about what they were doing, then call upon them to pool their ideas. At the very beginning of the year, *I* had to

supply some of the pooled questions but most pupils quickly learnt to offer appropriate questions themselves.

The fundamental assumption of teaching styles that use problem- solving is that pupils are *mathematical thinkers* in their own right, even if their thinking is not yet very advanced. What they think for themselves, and what they themselves discover, is based on their own understanding.

In traditional styles of teaching, pupils were regarded as 'empty vessels' into which mathematical skills had to be poured by the teacher. The growth of new technology, including calculators, computerised accounting systems, and computer- controlled machines, has meant that the traditional arithmetical and other skills, often learnt by rote, are now in little demand; the need is for people who can face, and cope with, an ever- changing variety of problems and situations.

National Curriculum mathematics

Trends in mathematics education and the National Curriculum

The National Curriculum in mathematics is laid down in a set of fourteen Attainment Targets, each of which is arranged in ten increasing levels of difficulty (DES and Welsh Office, 1989). A Statutory Instrument states the levels which apply at each key stage, as follows:

Key stage	Ages	Levels
Key stage 1	5- 7	1-3
Key stage 2	7-11	2-6
Key stage 3	11-14	3-8
Key stage 4	14-16	4-10

Each pupil is to be assessed on each Attainment Target at the end of each key stage. Teachers are required (with some exceptions as explained later) to teach in such a way that pupils should attain a level within the set of levels laid down for their key stage.

The Attainment Targets cover five areas of mathematical content, as follows:

Number
Algebra
measures
Shape and space
Handling data

Each content area is represented at each key stage, although at the early levels, *algebra* is concerned with number patterns, and traditional algebra does not appear until level 5. *Handing data* deals with topics which are of increasing importance in the modern world: the collection, presentation and analysis of statistical data, and the understanding of probability.

The five areas of mathematical content listed above occupy twelve of the fourteen Attainment Targets. The remaining two Attainment Targets (ATs 1 and 9) concern an important innovation in mathematics syllabuses, the topic of *using and applying mathematics.* In the National Curriculum, pupils are expected not only to learn mathematics, but also to be able to use it and apply it to a variety of situations. The Non-Statutory Guidance (National Curriculum Council, 1989a) states that:

Attainment Targets 1 and 9 provide objectives for pupils:

- acquiring knowledge, skills and understanding through practical work, through tackling problems and through using physical materials;
- applying mathematics to the solution of a range of 'real life' problems, and to problems drawn from the whole curriculum;
- exploring and investigating within mathematics itself.

(National Curriculum Council, 1989a, our emphasis)

Thus, the important recent trends in mathematics education described earlier which involve using *problem-solving* and *investigation* as major components of mathematics learning, have been incorporated into National Curriculum mathematics. These ways of working are of great importance to pupils with special needs in mathematics, because they help to ensure that mathematics can become a real tool in the pupils' lives.

The Non-Statutory Guidance encourages teachers to incorporate using and applying mathematics in all their mathematics learning, and not confine it only to work on Attainment Targets 1 and 9.

using and applying mathematics... should stretch across and permeate all other work in mathematics, providing both the means to, and the rationale for, the progressive development of knowledge, skills and understanding in mathematics. (National Curriculum Council, 1989a)

The Attainment Targets on using and applying mathematics are laid down in terms of three themes:

Using mathematics
Communicating in mathematics
Developing ideas of argument and proof

Using mathematics is concerned with planning the work on a task, reviewing progress, and checking that results are sensible. *Communicating in mathematics* concerns oral communication as well as writing and graphical work:

Record findings and present them in oral, written or visual form as appropriate. (DES and Welsh Office, 1989, ATs 1/9, level 4)

Developing ideas of argument and proof deals with the development of the pupil's mathematical thinking. It emphasises the making and testing of predictions, conjecturing, defining, proving and disproving:

Use examples to test statements or definitions. (ATs 1/9, level 4)

Hence, many elements of recent good practice in the teaching of mathematics fall under the heading of 'using and applying mathematics'. In this way, the National Curriculum should encourage the growth of good practice in mathematics teaching to pupils with special needs in mathematics, as well as to other pupils.

There is encouragement, too, for teachers to see mathematics as an element of cross-curricular work since they are encouraged to use *problems drawn from the whole curriculum*. This is not unduly difficult in primary schools, where there is already much cross-curricular topic or thematic work. In secondary schools it will demand co-operation and detailed discussion between different subject departments.

Another topic of importance to pupils with special needs in mathematics is the use of calculators, which will be important tools in their adult life. Here, too, the National Curriculum is likely to have a helpful influence. The Non-Statutory Guidance says:

The National Curriculum... requires pupils to develop a range of methods for calculating — from mental methods through to the use of electronic calculators... Calculators are now an established item of classroom equipment, and should be available for pupils to use at all four key stages... For most practical purposes, pupils will use mental methods or a calculator to tackle problems involving calculations. Thus the heavy emphasis placed on teaching standard written methods in the past needs to be re-examined. (National Curriculum Council, 1989a)

Several of the Attainment Targets require the use of a calculator:

> Solve problems involving multiplication or division of whole numbers or money, using a calculator where necessary. (AT 3, level 3)

> Read a calculator display to the nearest whole number. (AT4, level 4)

Thus, all pupils will need to know how to use a calculator, and how to incorporate its use into their mathematics. This will be very helpful to pupils with special needs in mathematics.

However, the National Curriculum's view of calculation has not completely moved into the era of new technology. Pupils are still required to carry out without calculators some tasks that seem to relate to pre-calculator methods of calculation.

> (Using whole numbers) understand and use non-calculator methods by which a 3-digit number is multiplied by a 2-digit number and a 3-digit number is divided by a 2-digit number. (AT3, level 5)

The approach of the Non-Statutory Guidance, that 'for most practical purposes, pupils will use mental methods or a calculator to tackle problems involving calculations' seems to be more in accord with the practice of most adults than does this Attainment Target. Indeed, some pupils with special needs in mathematics may find the need for a calculator when dealing with calculations at the level of:

> (Using whole numbers) add or subtract mentally two 2-digit numbers;... without a calculator add or subtract two 3-digit numbers, multiply a 2-digit number by a single-digit number and divide a 2-digit number by a single-digit number. (AT3, level 3)

It will probably take some years before calculators are completely accepted in schools, and by the National Curriculum, as the usual tools for doing calculations beyond the range of mental skill. Problems of acceptance in schools do not seem to arise with all aspects of modern technology; electric sewing machines, electric lathes and electronic computers have gained comparatively ready acceptance in schools, compared with the rearguard actions still fought against calculators in some schools.

Another recent, and important, emphasis in mathematics education is to ensure that pupils receive a broad curriculum in mathematics, and that their work does not over-emphasise some particular aspects, such as a narrow range of computational skills. The mathematics used in present-day adult life is much more varied; we saw earlier that many adults enlist the aid of others when they need to measure or read timetables, as most people do from time to time. The press and the media bombard us with statistical data, often in graphical form, and invite us to draw important conclusions. Shape and space are all around us, and knowledge of shape is required to carry out many jobs and hobbies.

The National Curriculum lays down a broad curriculum in mathematics, and will ensure that pupils with special needs in mathematics are not confined to a limited diet of number and computation. The National Curriculum Council, in *A Curriculum for All* 1989c) points out that:

> All pupils, including those with s.e.n., are entitled to participate in the National Curriculum and to derive the benefits of a broad and balanced mathematics education.

(National Curriculum Council 1989c)

However, the National Curriculum may create additional difficulties for teachers who work with pupils with SEN in mathematics. We now look briefly at some of those difficulties and how they may be alleviated.

Implementing the National Curriculum for pupils with SEN in mathematics

A problem which must exercise the minds of teachers of pupils with special needs in mathematics is the problem of meeting the needs of those very low-attaining pupils who do not attain at least level 1 by age 7, level 2 by age 11, level 3 by age 14, and level 4 by age 16. In fact, teachers are not required to work only within the range of levels laid down for each key stage, if those levels are not appropriate to the needs of the pupils concerned. The National Curriculum Council (1989c) quotes for guidance provided by the DES:

> It will be possible for pupils to be taught for part of the time (perhaps as much as half or more) at levels below those specified for their key stage, so long as they also work on programme of study material specified for their key stage during the latter part of the key stage.

(National Curriculum Council, 1989c) p.10)

Teachers will not know the results of trying to carry out this guidance for several years; by then, there will be more experience as to whether the present Attainment Targets are appropriate to the needs of low-attaining pupils in mathematics. However, it is not very likely that a pupil will have reached the same level in every Attainment Target, and it may well be possible to comply with the guidance — at least for some pupils — providing them with work appropriate to their key stage in those areas of mathematics in which they are most advanced and confident.

Pupils who need to work for most of their time below the levels specified may have these levels modified in a statement of special educational needs:

> Any pupils with statements of s.e.n. who need to be taught programme of study material for most or all of their time below the ranges specified may be exempted through their statement from the specified ranges...

Some pupils with severe learning difficulties may be working towards statements of attainment in Level 1 throughout most or all of their school days. If so their statements will need to modify the ranges of levels. (National Curriculum Council, 1989c p.10)

It is also possible that for a few pupils, probably those with some physical disabilities, the format of the Standard Assessment Tasks may be modified, or they might be disapplied. Guidance on the assessment of pupils with special educational needs is awaited.

The National Curriculum Council's guidance emphasises the importance of devising careful progressive schemes of work for those pupils who need a substantial amount of work below level 1. This is particularly important in mathematics, where the concepts and forms of language used in level 1 often rely on a substantial earlier build-up of concepts. To take a very few examples, consider the following Attainment Targets:

Select criteria for sorting a set of objects and apply consistently. (AT 12, level 1)

State a position using prepositions such as: on, inside, above, under, behind, next to, etc. (AT 11, level 1)

Children need much experience of handling and talking about sets of things which have likeness and differences, and experience of moving about the room and out of doors, and talking about what they are doing, in order to build up the necessary ideas to achieve these Attainment Targets. Some children acquire these ideas before the age of five: others do not. It will be necessary to ensure that both pupils and their parents are well-informed about any needed progressive schemes of work below level 1.

In conclusion, the most important feature of a curriculum for those pupils who have special needs in mathematics is that it should be *needs-driven*. The pupil's needs must continue to be paramount. For some pupils, their needs may not fit very comfortably alongside the mathematics Attainment Targets, but there is not yet enough experience of operating a National Curriculum to know whether this will be the case. In the meantime, it will remain the responsibility of the teacher to continue to provide the best possible education in mathematics for each pupil. Teachers should also keep careful records of children's attainments in mathematics, and how well these fit with the National Curriculum. These records will be needed as a component of the review and revision of the National Curriculum which will inevitably take place in the course of time.

References and Further Reading

Assessment of Performance Unit (1985) *A Review of Monitoring in Mathematics: 1978 to 1982,* London: HMSO.

Bird, M. (1983) *Generating Mathematical Activity in the Classroom,* Bognor Regis, West Sussex Institute of Higher Education.

Burton, L. (1984) *Thinking Things Through: Problem Solving in Mathematics,* Oxford: Basil Blackwell.

Denvir, B., Stolz, C., Brown, M. (1982) *Low Attainers in Mathematics 5-16: Policies and Practices in Schools,* (Schools Council Working Paper 72), London: Methuen Educational.

DES (1978) *Special Educational Needs: Report of the Committee of Enquiry into the Education of Handicapped Children and Young People,* [The Warnock Report], London: HMSO.

DES (1979) *Aspects of Secondary Education in England: a survey by HM Inspectors of Schools,* London: HMSO.

DES (1982) *Mathematics Counts: Report of the Committee of Inquiry into the Teaching of Mathematics in Schools under the Chairmanship of Dr W.H. Cockcroft,* [The Cockcroft Report] London: HMSO.

DES (1990) *Education Observed: Special Needs Issues: a Survey by HMI,* London: HMSO.

DES and Welsh Office (1989) *Mathematics in the National Curriculum,* London: HMSO.

Fisher, R. (Ed.) (1987) *Problem Solving in Primary Schools,* Oxford: Basil Blackwell.

Hart, K.M. (Ed.) (1981) *Children's Understanding of Mathematics: 11-16,* London: Blackwell.

Hart, K.M., Johnson, D.C. Brown, M., Dickson, L., Clarkson, R. (1989) *Children's Mathematical Frameworks 8-13: A Study of Classroom Teaching,* Slough: NFER-Nelson.

Haylock, D.W. (1986) 'Mathematics Low Attainers Checklist', *Br. J. Educ. Psychol.,* 56, 203-308.

Haylock, D.W. (1987) 'Towards Numeracy', *Support for Learning,* 2,2, 13-17.

Haylock, D.W. (1987) 'When things just don't add up', *Child International,* 77, pp.32-35.

HMI (1989) *A Survey of Pupils with Special Educational Needs in Ordinary Schools,* London: DES.

Jones, R.J. (1976) *The Usability of Mathematics Textbooks as Found in Third-Year Junior Classes,* M.Ed. thesis, Sheffield.

Larcombe, A. (1985) *Mathematics Learning Difficulties in the Secondary School: Pupil Needs and Teacher Roles,* Buckingham: Open University Press.

Larcombe, A. (1988) 'Mathematical: Prospects and Problems', Brit. J. of Special Education, 15, 4, pp.163-6.

Lewis, G. (1989) *'The Negotiated Curriculum: or One Thing Leads to Another', Struggle: mathematics for low attainers,* 24, Summer.

MESU (1989) *New Technology in Primary Mathematics: INSET Resources,* Coventry: MESU.

National Curriculum Council (1989a) *Mathematics: Non-Statutory Guidance,* London: NCC.

National Curriculum Council (1989c) *Curriculum Guidance 2: A Curriculum for All: Special Educational Needs in the National Curriculum,* London: NCC.

Shuard, H., Rothery, A. (Eds.) (1984) *Children Reading Mathematics,* London: John Murray.

Shuard, H., Walsh, A., Goodwin, J. and Worcester, V. (1990) *Children, Mathematics and Learning,* London: Simon & Schuster.

The Spode Group (undated) *Solving Real Problems with Mathematics,* Volume 1. Cranfield, CIT.

The Spode Group (1982) *Solving Real Problems with Mathematics,* Volume 2. Cranfield, CIT.

Watchman, W. (1990) 'Why the use of DART and Turtling are central to the provision of special needs education at the Ridge Junior School', *Micro-Scope, Special Education Special,* Summer 1990.

Chapter 6

History and children with special educational needs in the national curriculum

Peter Knight and Alan Farmer

Introduction

The National Curriculum is intended to deliver an entitlement curriculum to all children. As far as history is concerned this will be a radical innovation. In the infant years little history work is done (HMI 1989). In the junior years there is more, but the effective history curriculum is patchy, poorly organised and dominated by work on local and recent topics (Swift & Jackson 1987, HMI 1989). In the secondary years most children do history for three years, but only some 40% continue it in the fourth and fifth years (HWG 1989).

The History Working Group (HWG) was told that between 7.5% and 10% of the timetable should be given over to history. Its report (1990) required that a good range of topics was covered, planned that these topics should form a coherent and progressive set, and set ten levels of attainment for each of its three attainment targets. Unlike the Science and Geography Working Groups, the History Group did not set any attainment targets related to knowledge of specific history themes. In its report there is no historical equivalent of Light, Force, and World Geography, although the Historical Association has said that there could be attainment targets in Local, National and International history. However, as things stand in the National Curriculum document children's progress will be measured against their display of competence in general historical concepts and processes — namely: understanding time and causation; understanding points of view and historical interpretations; and locating, evaluating, using and drawing conclusions from primary and secondary sources. Children will also have to learn a lot of historical content but assessment of their content knowledge is *not* fundamental to the History programme.

Who has special needs?

Throughout the chapter, we use the term special educational needs in the broadest possible context. Almost all of what we say, therefore, is directed at the non-statemented pupils — if only because they are by far the greater number of children with such needs. As readers of this book recognise, many children have learning difficulties of a mild, moderate and often only temporary kind, sometimes accompanied with 'behavioural problems'. There is a variety of reasons for this — social deprivation, hearing and/or eyesight problems, emotional instability, immaturity, poor linguistic ability, poor attainment in reading and writing, a poor memory, a negative attitude to school, a low academic self-image etc. Moreover, these needs are not just a reflection of pupils' inherent difficulties. Needs vary over time and may be alleviated or exacerbated by many factors of which school policies and teaching is one. With this in mind, we recall the Scottish Education Department's 1978 estimate that up to 50% of children might have some special learning difficulty.

History too hard for pupils with special educational needs?

There is a view that history should not be taught to children with special needs because:

1. it is essentially a literary subject, beyond pupils who find it hard to read and write;

2. it is too difficult for many pupils, partly because the past cannot be directly observed, and partly because history is about the thoughts, deeds and emotions of adults living in 'strange' cultures;

3. even basic historical reasoning looks daunting for many children — it *can* be hard to get to grips with matters such as primary sources, bias, the imaginative reconstruction of the past, dealing with conflicting interpretations, analysis, inference, and judgement. Likewise, much of history's everyday language, for example *communism, factory, field, medieval, soldier.* Nor do we know how far children understand historical terms in senses very different from those which we intend.

However, we follow Bruner's claim that 'any subject can be taught effectively in some intellectually honest form to any child at any stage of

86

development' (Bruner, 1963, p.33). Truly this is a bold and problematic claim. We repeat it on the grounds that it embodied a vision of what could be. In that spirit we think that history is a 'splendid subject' and that all pupils should have 'an understanding of their own cultural roots and shared inheritances' (HWG, 1990, p.1).

The belief that history is appropriate for children with special educational needs is not idle: Blakeway (1983), Blyth (1988), Ashby and Lee (1987), Hallam (1984), Wilson (1985) and West (1981) have shown how children of modest achievement can undertake realistic, worthwhile history work. Here we are heartened by recent research which argues that effective schools advance the progress of all their pupils (Moretimore *et.al.,* 1988; Smith and Tomlinson, 1989). We risk the assumption that effective secondary school *departments* also help all pupils. This is important because in the early days of the new curriculum not many primary schools and secondary departments will make children with special educational needs their priority. The best we can expect, initially, is for general good history teaching, hoping that its magic will rub off on all. Good general history teaching is not a sufficient condition for successful history work with children with special educational needs, but it is certainly a necessary one. That is the assumption on which we write.

Is the national history curriculum too hard for children with special needs?

Writers on history and children with special educational needs have emphasised that the teacher should carefully tailor the curriculum to the child. The content outlined in the National Curriculum document (DES, 1991) and other structural features of the curriculum hamstring that advice. Teachers have had tremendous freedom to devise their own schemes of work, define their own targets for individual children, set their own tests/tasks and choose for which, if any, external examinations they should prepare and enter their pupils. When teaching history they have probably had more freedom than has been usual in 'the basics'. At best this has fertilised teachers' creativity and produced fine fruits.

But that free-range era is itself nearly history, and many are worried about what is to come. If the new curriculum is misconceived, then surely it is laughable to think of giving children with special educational needs access to it — should they not be protected from it?

Consider some of the criticisms:

1. Many primary teachers dislike the (perceived) secondary style of the history reports. They particularly dislike the single-subject approach which cuts at what many consider to be the heart of primary education — the child-centred, cross-curricular, integrated project/topic approach. Many teachers of children with special

educational needs share the same outlook and they have the same fears.

2. Many teachers are concerned at the amount of history to be covered.

3. The programme of study differ from what is normally taught now in the secondary phase. Research by both Helen Patrick (1987) and Spartacus publications has shown that there was already a common, secondary phase history curriculum. The HWG's choice of content (which arguably does not quite square with its own criteria) is the death knell of much existing good practice and a warning that new swathes of content will have to be mastered, especially by Key Stage 2 teachers (Knight, 1990, p.29).

4. The new attainment targets stand in a problematic relationship with the GCSE criteria which secondary teachers have just mastered.

5. If children are to succeed with the History curriculum, it should embody a sound view of child development in that domain. It is arguable that the HWG's levels of attainment, which constitute a developmental taxonomy, are vaguely expressed, frequently mis-conceived, and make distinctions without differences. Furthermore, there was ambiguity in the final report (HWG, 1990, p.117) as to whether progression was to be governed by the attainment target levels, by other general factors, or simply through covering more content.

6. The problems with assessment which were faced by the HWG were severe but not unique. they included the problems resulting from multiple statements about an attainment target level, problems of weighting, vague statements, and the tension between the norma-tive expectations of the government about the range of achievement and the criterion-referenced, and sometimes unrealistic, attainment target levels.

7. It is assumed that teachers will have the capacity and interest to communicate the richness of the past to all pupils. In the primary sector at least, there is a lack of relevant expertise (Knight, 1990).

Four specific fears about the curriculum and children with special educa-tional needs should also be noticed:

1. Schools will continue to design their own units of study and to write schemes of work within the National Curriculum framework. That involves mastering a whole new approach to the curriculum and it will not be surprising if it proves difficult; nor will it be surprising if the interests of minorities are marginalised in the process.

2. High-visibility assessment may damage even further the self- es-teem of children who are doing badly (in normative terms). What

some commentators have missed is that hitherto such damage could be confined to 'the skills', 'the morning subjects' — English, mathematics and maybe science. Now it is to be generalised. One teacher interviewed in a study of good practice in Key Stage 2 History said '... if you went to a class and said 'Are you good at Maths?' some would say yes and others would say no. If you said often 'Are you good at History?', that would throw them', because, as another said, (... the child who wasn't very good would go for History because you are not pin-pointed to quite the same extent: or in the words of a third 'the difficulties are more obvious in maths than they are in History. To them. They wouldn't realise they had difficulties, would they?' End of an era?

3. In Science one piece of advice about presenting the National Curriculum to children with special educational needs is to provide plenty of 'hands-on' activity (NCC, 1989). There are equivalents in history — handling artefacts, oral history, visits and fieldwork, modelling. They are most common in local history, since hands-on work with Egyptian mummies and interviews with Aztecs present some difficulties. The HWG proposals include many topics which offer few opportunities for 'hands-on' work.

4. The low priority given to special educational needs is a source of chagrin. The Interim Report ran to 120 pages and gave two paragraphs to the issue.

The benefits of the history national curriculum

The HWG was in an impossible position, dealing with one of the most culturally-central and contested subjects in the curriculum. Subtle though the report is, inevitably there have been cries of horror, and obviously a lot of sweat is going to be needed if children with special educational needs are to get much out of history in the 1990s. but what have the 1980s had to offer?

The present process of schooling does little for the self-esteem of many pupils. Too many pupils are still under-achieving; too little is expected of them; they are receiving insufficient and inappropriate help within the classroom. This is as true in history as in other subjects and of children with — as well as those without —special educational needs. HMI reports have often criticised the limited fare which many children with special educational needs receive in History: 'The whole history curriculum for the child of below-average ability is in need of serious revision; and this encompasses a broader band of children than the least able 10 or 15 percent (Wilson, 1985, p.17). Few history textbooks are simple linguistically and conceptually *and* mature and interesting. Unsurprisingly many pupils with special needs seem to have a 'relatively unfavourable attitude' (Wilson, p.14) to history in the 80s.

Perhaps it is as well that many children have done little 'history' at school.

Set against this picture, the National Curriculum, virtually irrespective of what it requires, has advantages. At least it should ensure the following:

1. There will be a structure for continuity and progression and less of the 'lucky dip' curriculum.

2. It will provide explicit and specific targets at which teachers and pupils can aim. The number of History attainment targets is manageable and understandable (especially compared to Mathematics and Science) and unlike Geography, the attainment targets are not made up of a tangle of strands.

3. Having specific — and relatively short-term — targets might motivate and give pupils a sense of achievement. At least Behaviourists would have us believe so!

4. Teachers and schools should feel obliged to get all children to reasonable levels — if only to satisfy the governors!

5. The requirement that all pupils should have access to the full curriculum *could* discourage schools from marginalising pupils with special educational needs.

6. The National Curriculum calls for observation and careful monitoring of the performances of all children, which makes sense when there is a formative intention behind it and where the data about children's developing (or stationary) understandings are subsequently used.

7. The HWG reports have emphasised the importance of differentiation.

8. Increased accountability *might* make clear the need for a whole-school approach to the teaching of special educational needs pupils, using school co-ordinators and specialist advice to plan the contributions that various subjects and activities can make.

9. Scope remains for teachers to determine their own approaches and ways of delivering their programmes. This will allow for responsiveness to individuals' needs and difficulties in learning. Teachers will also have room to choose History Study Units which they think will suit their pupils' needs, and they will be able to devise some HSUs themselves in Key Stages 2 and 3.

10. There is nothing inherently wrong in having a 'Plato to Nato' type approach, although it is not the only way of teaching children about time. It makes sense to many children, teachers and parents.

11. All children will be taught a reasonable amount of History, though the subject has been made optional in Key Stage 4. We conclude that even if this is not the national history curriculum which many wanted, and even if it is not the most suitable curriculum for

children with special educational needs, it is nonetheless a curriculum with some advantages, a curriculum which can be accommodated to the characteristics of English school children.

We now turn to ways of presenting a faulty curriculum effectively, with particular attention to ways in which craftful and crafty teaching may make it work with children with special educational needs.

Two assumptions

We make two assumptions about the working of this new curriculum;

1. In Humanities and topic work teachers have often catered for the range of abilities in the class through differentiation by outcome — by providing broadly similar activities for all in the expectation that children would engage with the activities in their own way, at their own level. The National Curriculum framework implies that teachers will increasingly set different tasks on a topic for different children, although the HWG report was carefully agnostic on ways of providing differentiated assessment. This differentiation by task does not necessarily require setting or streaming. A mixed ability class might be working on Attainment Target One, strand (a). Some might be concentrating on level 2, others on level 4 and others on level 5.

2. We also assume that resources will remain in short supply and that publishers will not see a market in history for children with special educational needs. Any increase in school staffing will be mopped up by organisational and assessment activities and not directed to children with special educational needs.

Making it interesting

Interest is invariably stressed as a key ingredient of history. The first aim of the GCSE National Criteria is that history courses should 'stimulate interest in the enthusiasm for the study of the past', and the HWG stressed the importance of 'interest, excitement, and enjoyment' (HWG, 1989, p.77).

Interesting topics do motivate. While we reject the idea that children with special educational needs are generally characterised by a lack of motivation, we do believe that they need a great deal of motivation to surmount their learning difficulties. Unfortunately, motivational theories are better at explaining what has happened than at predicting what will happen (rather like history!) and so they do not greatly help the teacher who is trying to choose interesting and motivating topics. Such a teacher will know that interest is variable: girls and boys, older and younger, introverts and extroverts may all have different interests.

So how are interesting topics to be chosen? A sample of 'good' primary teachers would no doubt incline to the view that any history topic could be interesting if presented well. That does not get us very far in terms of topics to be taught, but in the absence of relevant research, there is little else that can be done, apart from repeating that the vivid, dramatic and exotic do have a hold over the imagination. However, we can be more specific about interesting teaching approaches. For this we suggest the following principles:

1. Emphasise people: history is about people, not time, nor points of view, nor evidence.

2. Centre the topic on stories, presented as conflicts of people, forces or principles — albeit in simple forms. Here we have sympathy with the ideas of Egan (1979). He suggested that most children between the ages of about 4 and 9 years are at a mythic stage of development, thinking in ways redolent of the old myth-stories which are built on the conflict of opposites. He argues that story-form is a powerful way of organising any kind of content, especially for such children, and he says that stories have been underestimated in modern educational practices. The idea of a mythic stage is useful in planning lessons for some older children with special educational needs.

3. Look out for the dramatic detail, the telling piece of colour. Egan suggests that after the mythic stage, children want to explore the limits of the real world which 'suddenly' fascinates them. He argues that they enjoy the kind of content which fills the Guinness Book of Records. It is the strange and the bizarre that engages and is most accessible, not the near-at-hand and the local. This love of the bizarre, he says, is not some immature defect that needs to be repressed; rather it is a reflection of the profound truth that only when boundaries are known can one meaningfully chart details within them.

4. Therefore, do not assume that history which is in evidence in the children's immediate environment is interesting whereas the history of say, medieval England (which has left few traces in many areas and fewer still which are accessible to children) is uninteresting. Arguably, that claim makes as much sense if it is completely stood on its head! Nor is there much truth in the claim that local, recent content is concrete (in the sense in which the Piagetian idea is commonly misunderstood) while other content is not.

Teaching points

We think that teaching styles, methods and resources are more important in motivating children than the best-conceived syllabus. The HWG has given some indication of what they consider to be good practice in teaching methods, but they hardly go beyond the pious hopes and clichés. Here we sketch eight teaching points which we think can enhance motivation and which may do much to bridge the gap between the content of the National Curriculum and the child with special educational needs. We make it clear that several of these approaches are replete with problems.

1. *'Hands-on' History.* It is desirable that children handle things from the past, although assumptions that this sort of physical activity *necessarily* leads to mental activity are severely mistaken, a point which is accepted by Piaget's Genevan school of epistemology and psychology. Agreed, the thrill of 'hands-on' history is almost reason enough for doing it, but if children are to advance their grasp of attainment target levels, close attention must be given to its purpose and structure.

    For example, a mixed age class of children in Key Stage 1 is working with old- and new-stone-age axes, replica bronze age weapons, victorian and modern toys. They work in groups and considerable emphasis has been put on the socialisation aspect of insisting on certain fair ways of working together. The intention is that they should apply a limited, historical vocabulary (which was developed earlier in the week) and that they should look, systematically, for clues about the identity and use of the artefacts. While the session has a lot of 'buzz-time', it also has a structure, since the children are working with a small deck of prompt cards. Turn one over and it asks *the group* to decide 'what was it used for?'. Others ask them to say whether certain adjectives — pitted, worn, heavy — fit the artefact.

    Notice that in this example (which is based upon the work of Dr J. West) there is a purpose, a mixture of free and structured talk about the artefact, and, arguably, a greater contribution to the English curriculum than to History.

2. *Visits and Fieldwork.* The HWG has stressed the virtues of field-work and visits. Indeed the interim report (HWG, 1989) emphasised this so much that it could have given the impression that the curriculum would be delivered by fieldwork. Broadly speaking, the points made in (1) above apply. Unless a considerable amount of time has been spent in briefing and preparation, there is evidence that children do not benefit from visits in the way envisaged. Pond's research (1983) showed that many children (and probably many adults!) simply see a pile of stones when they visit Kits Coty, Housesteads or Fountains Abbey. They find it difficult to imagine the site as it was *lived* in its prime. More able pupils benefited more from visits, said Pond, because they were able to *imagine* the past from the surviving evidence. So, for children with special educational needs, enormous teaching skill and insight are needed if

school visits are to be a particularly useful aid to understanding (although they might fail on that criterion and yet succeed by creating a general, favourable disposition towards history).

Fieldwork is time-consuming, it can interfere with the timetable of other subjects and it can be expensive.

3. The HWG (1989) commended *'drama, role-play, re-enactments, simulations and related approaches'* as methods of 'considerable potential' in giving pupils 'insight into the behaviour of people in the past and into their motivation, reactions and relationships' (p.78). There has been considerable emphasis placed on gaming/simulation techniques since the 1950s. They were then seen as a panacea — especially in the USA. There are few history simulations, and — with notable exceptions, such as those by Jordan and Wood, — fewer good ones. Even where the computer is used to ease the complexity of running simulations, most are complicated, and require children to have good memories and reading skills.

    We have a firm belief in the power of drama in history learning but we have an equally firm belief that teachers need special skills to succeed. The pageant and performance side of drama, where children mime out a story (and perhaps mutter a few words) is not without value, but there is so much more that can be achieved with children of all ages and abilities if the teacher is able to draw on a battery of specialist techniques to get them thinking as they work with historical problems and to get them understanding something of the logic behind the actions of people in the past. This is not the place to unpack the idea of drama and history education. The work of Fines and Verrier (1974) is seminal and, we think, persuasive. Unfortunately this way of using drama takes time to learn and time to do in a crowded curriculum. Moreover, many teachers rightly apprehend that if they are going to lose control of a group it will be during drama.

4. Attention to the language curriculum. This point scarcely needs making. Effective special educational needs teaching takes heed of the National Curriculum for English, involves collaboration with colleagues who have expertise in language development, and is sensitive to questions of audience, register, media, readability and the like. However, for many secondary schools it will be a major innovation to achieve this effective integration of English and history — let alone for the children with special educational needs. And in some primary classrooms, language expertise is deployed in 'English' time, not in 'Geography', 'Science' or 'History' time. 'Language across the curriculum' can be a platitude and not a description of practice.

5. *Questioning styles.* Again it is a common claim that many of the questions which teachers ask (in print and orally) are obscure ('read my mind'), trivial, and tap a narrow range of mental abilities. Again, the remedies are ostensibly simple but practically complex. Received wisdom is to ask more open-ended questions, but considered responses to these questions depend on having information on which to base an opinion, otherwise we encourage the notion that any opinion is as good as any other. Therefore, good questioning involves a mixture of informing, using closed questions to involve children, consolidation of essential points and then asking more, open-ended, questions.

Hargreaves (1984) has observed that this is the way many teachers work, and suggests that there should be scrutiny of the received wisdom that says that open questions are 'good', whereas closed questions are 'bad': each can have its place. If that is so, then the focus needs to be on the chains of questions that we ask, not upon individual questions. It matters that each chain is worthwhile and put together in a way which children can follow.

6. *Timelines.* Children need to be taught central ideas about time (AT1), not because history is about time, but because time is a filing system which allows us to arrange the great heap of information about the past. It is an important organisational idea which tells us what goes where, and what goes with what, but it is no more the quintessence of History than maps are the quintessence of Geography. So, children have to learn where patches of the past lie in the past, just as they have to learn where places are located on the globe. Timelines of some sort are necessary. They need to be devised with care and used with insight.

7. *The visual dimension.* Discounting obvious problems with partially-sighted children, we argue that visual sources have enormous power. 'A verbal rendering of concrete detail', notes P.J. Rogers, 'is feeble compared to what can be achieved by visual means' (Rogers, 1979).

The enlarging photocopier and licensing agreements have ensured that teachers can get mass copies of drawings and photographs which can provide a very effective way of using primary sources with children so that most levels of thinking in attainment target AT3 can be tackled (and some of targets 1 & 2 also). Reading difficulties need not get in the way of historical thinking.

We urge teachers to build up, purposefully, substantial banks of copies of primary and secondary visual sources and to use these to give children with reading difficulties access to levels of attainment which would otherwise be denied them.

Just as important as the 'still' image is film (Farmer, 1986). Indeed, now that the 1956 copyright act has been laid to rest, teachers can be swamped by the wealth of film that is available — feature films, general output programmes and school educational programmes. Some teachers are critical of TV and video. We accept that TV is not the attraction it once was for pupils. It is vital that teachers control the medium and are not controlled by it. They need to be clear about their aims and objectives in using film. Careful previewing is essential. appropriate activities (which need not be written) should be provided for children to engage in, both during and after the programme. It matters that the teacher 'build up' the film beforehand and places it in some kind of context. American research suggests the obvious: that film is most effective when used by good teachers: it is not a 'cure-all'. But we still believe that film can sustain attention and interest in a way that no other medium can. It can help bring remote events and people to life. It can provide a common educational experience that pays little heed to levels of ability. Films, especially feature films, can be biased and inaccurate. But bias and inaccuracy can be used by the history teacher as the whole subject of the video exercise. Use of film can be an excellent way of getting across difficult concepts like bias. Pupils often find it easier and pleasanter — to evaluate film critically than they do other types of historical evidence.

8. *Storytelling.* There is far less emphasis now on storytelling in history than there was in the past. In part this may be due to the influence of the Schools Council History Project and 'New' History which emphasised the importance of sources and which tried to turn children into mini-researchers. In part it may be because storytelling smacks of chalk and talk. At present it tends to be assumed that if children are not handling sources they are not doing history; if they are not busy doing they are not learning; if they are not involved in group interaction something is wrong: but there is also a place for story.

Storytelling (we prefer storytelling to story reading, which we think can lack immediacy) is especially important with children who have not mastered the skills of reading and writing. Many other children find the printed page lacks the sparkle and excitement of a spoken story. A good story/anecdote can enrich their imagination and help them to see things from the point of view of people in the past. It may also be an important way of helping children develop the concept of causality. Stories, after all, are about what people did, why they did things and what happened as a result.

The notion that children can only listen effectively for a few minutes at a time is something of an old wife's tale. If the story and story-teller are good enough, children will listen, albeit not indefinitely.

A good storytelling session depends on the harmony of three things; the story itself; the qualities of the story-teller; and the nature of the audience. Good stories need strong plots, a few main characters, plenty of action, drama and suspense, colourful background detail, and humour. It is, of course, essential that in telling the story the teacher should not be disrespectful of the truth — but we incline to the view that it is more important to get the spirit of the story right rather than the detail.

Good story-tellers come in all shapes and forms, each with their own idiosyncracies, styles and qualities. But a good memory — and faith and interest in the story are essential. The best story-teller, armed with the best story, has to take into account the nature of the audience — age, sophistication, and interests, and will watch them as the story is told, adjusting pace, tone and texture according to their responses. In this way children have considerable control over the story they are receiving. Storytelling is communal — a constant interaction between the teller and the audience.

Stories can be free standing. Usually, however, a story will be followed up in a variety of ways — discussion, individual or group research, drawing, drama etc. A story can be an excellent stimulus, providing a way into a topic. It can also run over several lessons, with (pictorial) source-based work and finding out activities interspersed. The teacher may pause part way through a story and ask children to predict what will happen next: mismatches between what they predict and what did happen can be exploited later. Through story children can be introduced to ideas, enthusiasms and thoughts in a way they can understand and which gives them enjoyment, insight and fun.

In conclusion

Those teaching history in the primary and secondary years are about to 'shoot Niagara' — and they don't know what to expect. In the primary sector there is a lack of expertise in good history practice, and in both sectors there is evidence that, even in the basics, it is hard to match the work to the understandings of the lower-achieving child. Time and money are in short supply, while no suitable published materials are yet available. We have noted other problems with the National History Curriculum.

Yet Nostradamus-like predictions are always chancy. This new curriculum may soon become domesticated and the National Curriculum document

(DES, 1991) gives teachers quite a lot of room to manoeuvre, so it is impossible to see what may be.

Inevitably, though, there are demanding times ahead. How, then, are schools and departments to implement this history curriculum and tune it to some children's special needs without ruining teachers' health?

Collaborative approaches to curriculum implementation become essential. If LEAs and schools utilise the LEATGS funds and training days imaginatively: if different groups of teachers each concentrate on particular aspects of curriculum implementation and share their findings; if the 'divide and rule' strategy of LMS is subverted; and if secondary school departments talk to each other and plan for integrated approaches to common concerns, just as primary curriculum co-ordinators should: then an imperfect curriculum may be beaten into shape which allows many children with special educational needs to handle matters of cultural centrality which have hitherto often been put beyond their grasp. But, without collaboration those children are likely to experience the snags in the history curriculum, not its benefits.

References

Ashby, R. and Lee, P.J. (1987) 'Discussing the Evidence', *Teaching History,* 48. pp.13-17

Blakeway, S.E. (1983) *Some Aspects of the Historical Understanding of Children aged 7-14,* London University, Unpublished MA dissertation

Blyth, J. (1988) *History 5-9,* Sevenoaks: Hodder and Stoughton.

Blyth, J. (1989) *History in Primary Schools,* Milton Keynes: Open University Press.

Blyth, W.A.L. (1990) *Making the Grade in Primary Humanities,* Milton Keynes: Open University Press.

Bruner, J. (1963) *The Process of Education,* New York: Vantage.

Department of Education and Science (1991) *History in the National Curriculum,* London: HMSO.

Egan, K. (1979) *Educational Development,* New York: Oxford University Press.

Farmer, A. (1986), Video and History, *Teaching History* 45, 9-13.

Fines, J. and Verrier, R. (1974) *The Drama of History,* London: New University Education.

Hallam, R.N. (1984) 'Robin Hood: History for Children with Learning Difficulties', *Education 3-13* 12:1, pp.40-46.

Hargreaves, D. (1984) 'Teachers' questions: open, closed and half-open', *Educational Research* 26:1 pp.46-51.

Her Majesty's Inspectors of Schools (1989) *The Teaching and Learning of History and Geography,* London: DES

History Working Group (1989) Interim Report, *London: DES*

History Working Group (1990) *Final Report, London: HMSO*

Knight, P.T. (1990) 'Inset, Research and the National Curriculum: the Case of History in Key Stages 1 & 2', *British Journal of Inservice Education,* 16:1, pp.27-32

Mortimore, P. (1988) *School Matters: the Junior Years,* Shepton Mallet: Open Books

Patrick, H. (1987) *A Report of a Survey of School History,* Leicester: Leicester University School of Education

Pond, M. (1983) 'School History Visits and Piagetian Theory', *Teaching History* 37, pp.3-6

Rogers, P.J. (1979) *The New History: Theory into Practice,* London: Historical Association.

Smith, D.J. and Tomlinson, S. (1989) *The School Effect,* London: Policy Studies Institute

Swift, R. and Jackson, M. (1987) *History in the Primary School,* Chester: Chester College of Higher Education

West, J. (1981) *History 7-13,* Dudley: Dudley Teachers Centre.

Wilson, J. (1985) *History for pupils with Learning Difficulties,* Sevenoaks: Hodder and Stoughton

Chapter 7

Geography for pupils with Special Education Needs

Nigel Proctor

Introduction

In this chapter I will attempt to answer the question 'of what possible use can geography be to the child with special educational needs?' I shall do this bearing in mind the needs, interests and concerns of children, especially those with special educational needs; the needs of teachers and students about methods and approaches to improve the enliven the teaching of geography, and why geography is of benefit to all pupils whether or not they have special educational needs. First, I want to examine the range of decisions made by the Government which led eventually to the inclusion of geography in the National Curriculum.

Geography And The DES Aims Of Schools

During the last years of the Labour government the DES issued a set of eight 'Aims of Schools' (DES, 1977) to guide debate about the curriculum for *all* schools. The last of the aims, as most teachers concerned with special needs will know, required schools 'to encourage and foster the development of all children whose social or environmental disadvantages cripple their capacity to learn, if necessary by making additional resources available to them'. Unfortunately this aim, with its necessary funding implications, was omitted when the list was revised and published (DES, 1980) under a Conservative government.

schools which *did* survive from the DES (1977) document
ctly concerns geographical education is 'to help children
e world in which we live and the interdependence of nations'.
(1990) list the aim was improved by addition of the words '...
s and groups'. Now we would surely all agree that this aim —
particularly with its emphasis on interdependence — is a fundamental
purpose in educating any child. But it is particularly important for children
with special needs, for we should recall that the Warnock Report (DES,
1978) had advocated a curriculum for these children which included essential knowledge 'about the world in which they are growing up.'

If we agree that these aims are important, we must surely concede that
'geo-graphy' — literally 'the description of the world' — becomes an
essential subject of study for all children. We need to demonstrate to pupils
that, despite all the worries they might have about their own lives, and
exacerbated by concerns about such issues as pollution, inequality and
exploitation, the world in which we live is still wonderful, or, more descrip-
tively, full of wonder. One geography professor (Paterson, 1979) pleaded
with teachers, 'Let us welcome anything which will increase that opportunity to wonder, and to weep, over the world of man'. The development of
a passion for the earth — termed 'topophilia' by the President of the
Association of American Geographers (Lewes, 1985) is, to my mind, one of
the essential aims of teaching geography to all children. Children whose
'social or environmental disadvantages cripple their capacity to learn' (DES,
1977) — more than others — are particularly entitled to such opportunities
for study.

There are other aims of schools to which geography usually contributes.
For instance, the DES (1980) believes that we should help *all* children 'to
appreciate how the nation earns and maintains its standard of living and
properly to esteem the essential role of industry and commerce in this
process'. It would need an economics graduate in *every* school to ensure this
aim is adequately met, though even then few would want to use the word
'esteem' about the role of industry, given its record on employment, im-
proper financial dealings and pollution of air, water and earth. More realistically, geographers will be expected to contribute to teaching about industry,
and the inclusion of economic geography in the National Curriculum is in
line with this need. Geography can also help schools meet other aims, such
as the development of children's understanding about other peoples' cultures, values and ways of life, and of their intellectual and communication
skills. We shall return to this issue after considering the value of geography
as a foundation subject when the special needs curriculum is being planned.

The curricular value of geography
Some 30 years ago, Tansley and Gulliford (1960), writing about special
needs dismissed a watered-down academic curriculum as a 'travesty of

special educational treatment'. Yet today the National Curriculum comprises ten separate and exclusive academic subjects, each with clear study and assessment programmes. Many of these including geography are so content-based that they must appear daunting for children with special needs.

Yet geography has many attractions when a special needs curriculum is being considered and planned because of the breadth of its content. It is an inter-disciplinary subject in its own right. When Sir Keith (now Lord) Joseph, then Secretary of State for Education, addressed the Geographical Association, he suggested that 'geographers themselves have to be clear about what their subject is *uniquely* or best qualified to offer, since it is on this basis that the subject's claim for scarce curriculum time should be made and judged'. Reference to 'uniqueness' in curriculum content is unusual, for such properties are rare, but Sir Keith identified one of geography's strengths in being 'a bridge between the humanities and the sciences'. The subject is, however, even broader than that, since it provides a wide coverage of three of the essential elements of the curriculum: science (particularly earth science), humanities (including perspectives ranging from anthropology to demography and sociology), and mathematics (including topology and simple techniques such as sampling and correlation). Interdisciplinary programmes rarely provide such breadth, being restricted to groupings of 'like' subjects, such as humanities or creative arts.

Despite this breadth, geography still provides a discipline, with all the educational benefits that term implies, such as an established and accepted purpose and rationale and a sequential framework for developing skills, particularly in mapwork and fieldwork. The discipline derives from restricting the subject to a spatial dimension and perspective comparable to history's temporal focus. Children of all abilities can recognise and appreciate this focus.

My argument is, therefore, that geography provides genuine benefits for those planning special needs curricula. The breadth and variety of its content, even though restricted to a spatial perspective, provide real opportunities for studies which can generate both interest and enthusiasm. Some children with special needs will be particularly motivated when these studies are drawn from the local environment (included in AT2 in the National Curriculum geography Order,) tackling issues of genuine concern and interest to the local community. It should be remembered that the cross-curricular component of the National Curriculum, advocated by both the DES (1989) and the NCC (1989) includes environmental education. For children with special needs these studies should realistically be drawn from the local area. Geographical study can also contribute to the development of other cross-curricular activities, particularly the development of children's language and numeracy skills. But the key contribution of geography to developing children's skills is in 'graphicacy' — the graph of geo-graphy — which has been identified by the NCC whole curriculum working group as an important cross-curricular area. It is to this issue that we now turn our attention.

Geo-graphy Contribution to Child Development

We are all aware that children — particularly those with special needs — are equipped with wide-ranging abilities. Over 20 years ago, Guilford's (1967) 'structure of intellect theory' indicated that there are at least 120 separate kinds of intellectual ability, of which everyone is likely to have at least one developed to a higher level than others. This classification has been of little use to curriculum planners for special needs because of its sheer complexity; indeed educational psychology as a whole has never played a key role in any public debate about the curriculum (Proctor, 1985a).

But all this could change with the publication of a book, applauded by Jerome Bruner, entitled *Frames of Mind: the theory of multiple intelligences* in which Gardner (1984) demonstrates that we have five separate intelligences, rather than merely abilities. His framework of the mind comprises the verbal, the logico-mathematical, and musical, the spatial and the bodily-kinaesthetic intelligences. Gardner criticises the over-emphasis in all schools on the verbal and the mathematical intelligence and argues that *all* children should be encouraged to acquire and develop a wider range of skills and abilities.

The inclusion of a *spatial* intelligence is particularly important when considering the role of geography and the curriculum for pupils with special needs. Spatial intelligence, highly developed in navigators, Eskimos and artists, is closely related to the communication skill of graphicacy, described as 'the communication of spatial information that cannot be conveyed adequately by verbal or numerical means' (Balchin, 1965).

We are all aware that children vary greatly in their spatial and graphicate ability, and this may be particularly noticeable in pupils with special needs. A classic example of outstanding drawing ability, combined with severe learning difficulties, is that of Steven Wiltshire, the autistic, brain-damaged boy featured in recent television documentaries. His remarkable drawing ability — including perfect perspective — was recognised by psychologists when he was six years old, and he has now published two books of drawings. Yet he was severely handicapped in every other intelligence.

A more 'everyday' example might be the work of a ten-year old we shall call 'Martin', who was asked to write an imaginative story on travel. The content of the essay was extremely good but Martin had specific learning difficulties and could not communicate effectively his ideas, or fully demonstrate his creativity and intelligence (his IQ was 140). But Martin could read (reading age 7.6 yrs) and he could draw accurately. At one time educational psychologists commonly used the Goodenough 'Draw a man' test to help gauge a child's intelligence; the accuracy and detail of showing parts of the body gained points, which were matched against age to provide a score, indicating spatial intelligence. Although recognised still as a classic example of a culture-free test (Valletutti, 1989) its accuracy has been questioned. Most of Martin's sketches and maps are accurate, neat and detailed. Unfortunately, as Gardner and other psychologists confirm, pref-erence is given to children with high levels of ability only in numeracy and literacy and, where children are alienated from these two areas, they find it difficult to demonstrate their intelligence and creativity (Lorac and Weiss, 1981).

If these dangers are to be prevented we need to ensure that some balance is achieved between the various communication skills. Since virtually all 'special needs' are in fact communication needs, this becomes an important element in the education of children with special needs and should be built into any curriculum framework. This approach is now developed.

Communication Skills, Graphicacy and a Special Needs Curriculum

In its report (DES, 1978), the Warnock Committee argued that the develop-ment of 'language' was the major requirement of the special needs curricu-lum, though a fairly narrow definition, restricted to literacy and oracy, was probably intended. In an article 'Writing a special needs curriculum state-ment' (Proctor, 1987) I have attempted to justify the adoption of a framework comprising five 'languages' or forms of communication, as follows:

Forms of Communication			
Mode of Communication	Form of Language	Productive Element	Receptive Element
Literacy	Written Language	Writing	Reading
Oracy	Spoken Language	Speaking	Listening
Numeracy	Number Language	Number manipulation and calculation	Number
Graphicacy	Graphic Language	Sketching and map making	Map and picture reading
Physiognomy	Body and Sign Language	Movement, Dance and Expression	Watching and interpreting

These five 'languages' resemble very closely the five areas which Tansley and Gulliford (1960) identified as the components of a genuine curriculum for special needs: written and oral language, number, creative and practical work and physical education. Religious education was added because of the statutory requirements. The five languages differ in that they focus entirely on the *skill* of communication, which is, to my mind, the most important aspect of education for children with special needs. As Wilson (1981) states: 'Planning the curriculum with special relation to basic skills is particularly relevant to special schools, because their pupils so often have to be taught in schools, skills which other children acquire naturally in the family situation'. The five languages do represent the 'basics' (Proctor, 1985b) in that they underpin all education; without these skills a person is disadvantaged practically, emotionally and academically. The five languages merely extend the cross-curricular approach advocated by Bullock's language (literacy and oracy) across the curriculum (DES, 1975) and Cockcroft's numeracy across the curriculum (DES, 1982). Indeed, cross-curricularity is now a fundamental aim of the National Curriculum, emphasised by both the DES (1989) and by the National Curriculum Council. Specifically Circular No.6 (NCC, 1989) identified cross-curricular communication skills as oracy, literacy, numeracy and graphicacy. The inclusion of graphicacy is important for it should encourage all teachers, not just those teaching geography, to focus upon developing in all children a range of skills which will be useful in their future lives. The framework is now used to exemplify some teaching strategies for special needs in geography lessons.

Literacy in the Geography Lesson

Reading:

The sentence length and vocabulary in the typical geography textbook will create difficulties for the child with special needs and the teachers needs to ensure that key sentences or passages from the book are read aloud, with intermittent questioning to check comprehension. Provided the teacher also checks the readability of the textbooks, there are clear advantages if children who are withdrawn from class continue to use the same book as mainstream pupils, so that they remain familiar with it, and confident about using it, particularly with the onset of the National Curriculum. Differentiated worksheets can produce very encouraging results in terms of both reading and writing, though, as with any other teaching method, over-use can lead to boredom. The worksheets need to be designed with care (Hartley, 1988) and have plenty of variety if reading and later writing skills are to be encouraged. The following are some suggestions:

   a. *Word searches,* where the page is full of letters; children encircle the word, e.g. a geographical term or location, arranged horizontally, vertically or diagonally. The problem is that it takes half an hour to produce an exercise which the quicker children finish in five minutes.

   b. *Jumbled words* or anagrams where children have to unscramble the word and write a sentence showing its meaning.

   c. *Crosswords,* with fairly simple clues e.g. 'A church with a spire is shown on OS maps as... Spare boxes can be used for sketches or symbols.

d. *Word columns,* where lists of commonly descriptive words are provided which children have to sort into different columns, e.g. a group of 30 weather words would be sorted into four columns — sun/cloud, precipitation, wind, or temperature.

e. *Missing words* (close procedure), where gaps are left in a text of two or three paragraphs, with a jumbled list of the correct words, together with some distractors to prevent guessing at the bottom of the page. This prevents unfortunate errors; one geography method book, for instance, has a sentence about an Italian monastery, with a sentence 'Most Italians are... 'which could lead to quite different interpretations, apart from 'Roman Catholics'!

f. *Matching sentences,* where a number of half-sentences, beginning and ending, are provided and children are asked to match the first half of a sentence with the correct second half — a technique encouraging careful reading and analysis, before children write down the full sentence.

Writing:

Children with special needs should be encouraged to develop a geographical vocabulary, by discussing and defining geographical terms before including them in their own sentences in their geography vocabulary book.

Sentence construction is difficult for, and geographical essays are quite beyond, younger children with special needs whose work needs to be carefully sequenced. The labelling of a diagram or completion of missing words are useful starters, followed by annotation of features on a map or sketch in surrounding boxes provided. More able children, incidentally, will be able to write more detailed sentences in the boxes, provided the boxes are big enough. Notes can be introduced gradually, usually from a blackboard summary of key words. Written answers to blackboard questions are rarely done well unless children are told either to write out the question, or to ensure that the meaning of their written answer is evident. It is commonly better to ask the class to complete a sentence, such as 'Wheat is grown on farm x because...' rather than 'Why is wheat grown on farm x?'. Some imaginative writing can be introduced so that children can see that creativity is valued as much as technical writing ability. Finally, a formal essay can be attempted, but only after discussion, leading to a blackboard summary of keywords and of instructions on the sequencing and composition of each paragraph.

Writing can be improved greatly by asking children to produce rough drafts before they attempt the final, polished version. Few adults can present written work without first planning and drafting, yet children are rarely given this opportunity (Hull, 1985). Their first attempts commonly stand as the finished essays, resulting in low marks and disillusionment. Again, most geography teachers recognise the importance of careful marking of children's written work, yet rarely discuss the purpose, techniques or detail of marking. This may become more crucial as records of achievement and pupil profiles appear in most schools. Practical advice on marking is provided elsewhere (Proctor, 1985c).

Oracy

The spoken word is the chief means by which all children, particularly pupils with special educational needs, communicate with their peers and with adults. Important though the written word is, most communication takes place in speech; and those who do not listen with attention and cannot speak with clarity, articulateness and confidence are at a disadvantage in almost every aspect of their personal, social and working lives.

Listening:

American and British research (e.g. Barnes, 1976) has found that talk takes up two-thirds of average lesson time and that two-thirds of this is teacher-talk, with the children as listeners.

Children with special needs have to learn how to listen attentively, and teachers can help by thinking carefully about the length, complexity and clarity of their expositions and questions. Moreover, they need to check that all children are listening in the first place. The child who is expected to answer the question could be named at the beginning: 'Damian, can you tell me why...?' Alternatively, the teacher's instruction 'Put your hands up if you know...' not only prevents shouting out of answers but enables him/her to gauge the extent, and reasons for, confusion; was it the way the question was phrased, the content, a previous absence or loss of memory?

Questions should be short and concise. I well remember one student teacher asking a large class of older boys with special needs a long, rambling and complex question about occupations of people living in the blighted, 'twilight' zone encircling the local city; one boy shouted out 'Prostitutes' to which the student teacher replied 'See me at the end of the lesson'. This would have been fine had it kept the answer coming in, but another had shouted out 'He wants to know where they all hang out, Tom'! The student quickly learned the value of planning lead questions carefully!

In geography lessons, pupils with special needs should have the opportunity of listening to accounts of different cultures, either a speaker from distant places or a tape recording of him/her. A number of my students have brought in friends who have travelled extensively or lived in the country being taught. Impact can result from a tape recording of a song with a message — such as 'Day Trip to Bangor' or 'The Streets of London' (see Renwick, 1981). Radio broadcasts can be taped. One of the most absorbing, poignant recordings I have used with children with special needs is that by a survivor of the Bangledesh disaster of 1970 from a 'Newsweek' interview by Maynard Parker:

It was like the end of the world,' Nomohan Das, 40, a farmer, recalled. 'About 6 o'clock we heard an extreme-danger signal over our radio and the wind began to blow. We tried to reach a storm shelter. The wind was so fierce that my wife and I and our six children made a human chain and tried to crawl on our hands and knees. But we couldn't make it. We had to turn back to my brother's house. The wind was blowing but we boosted each other onto the roof. It was raining. Three or four hours passed; then we heard a roar like it was the end of the world and the tidal wave was on us:

'The roof of the house ripped loose' Das went on. 'I grabbed my youngest son. The foot was floating and I grabbed a tree and held on for hours. I was freezing from the rain. Children would be swept by, screaming for help. I tried to grab onto them and tie them to me but the current was too strong. They were swept away. I felt helpless. About dawn the water began to go down. I could see bodies, hundreds of the, floating out to sea. At about 9 in the morning the water finally went down all the way. My farm looked like a desert. There was nothing left, but my family was all right. Only my Aunt had been washed away along with most of the old people. They were not strong enough to hold onto the trees. My son did not talk for hours. It was like he was dead. Finally, in the afternoon he sat down and just began to cry.

I have found that this account is so moving that even the most disruptive or uninterested child wants to know how such a thing could happen and is prepared to read about and discuss the whole sequence of climatic events which can lead up to the formation of a hurricane. Pupils with special needs, perhaps more than others, need to be motivated by the teacher, or they will contribute little to the lesson. This aspect is now considered.

Speaking:

Pupils with special needs must learn that the ideas they express orally are just as valid and valued as the same ideas when written: They might be encouraged for instance, to present reports for their work on a tape-recording. They need encouragement to contribute orally, perhaps first in small discussion groups, preparing an oral report to the whole class. The best topics are those which are controversial, with a problem-solving or hypothesis-testing approach, so common at GCSE level, or a role-playing simulation. Local examples might concern an inquiry into the building of a new motorway or hypermarket. More distant examples might develop empathy: 'How would *you* feel as an Amazon Indian if developers wanted to build a highway through *your* tribal land?'

Some teachers may experiment with drama to develop children's talk (Earish, 1985) outlines reconstructions of physical changes in snow, ice and glaciation, while one of my students has used children to dramatise the erosion of a sea cliff.

Numeracy

The Cockcroft Report (DES, 1982) urges the use of cross- curricular work in numeracy for all children, and this is particularly important for children with special needs, who may experience great difficulty understanding simple mathematical concepts, such as scale, time and measurement. Many of these are linked with graphicacy, in which the work should be carefully sequenced. Block graphs, where one unit is represented by one square, should precede the teaching of bar graphs, which require an understanding of vertical scale (Boardman, 1986). Liaison with the children's mathematics teacher may improve work on maps, involving scale, contours and direction.

Numeracy skills can be developed through fieldwork, which involves the collection, recording, analysis and evaluation of statistical data. Traffic counts commonly result in the production of bar graphs, showing the number of different vehicles using the road, but they could be used to test the hypotheses, say, that the particular road is overcrowded and should be improved, or by-passed. Traffic is graded as PCUs or Passenger Car Units — ½ PCU for a cycle or motor cycle, 1 PCU for a car or van, 2 PCU for a lorry and 3 PCU for a HGV. The use of statistics and quantitative techniques to analyse local, controversial issues is preferable to their use in the study of abstract mathematical and conceptual ideas which may be beyond the capability of SEN children. These methods were over-used in the 1960s, as indicated by Peterson (1979): 'In our preoccupation with strict empirical thought and method, we have short-changed several generations of students by giving them the model rather than the reality.'

The current 'revolution' in geography is the application of the computer, which introduces a whole new dimension to learning, and, properly used, can have great potential for children with special needs — particularly in reinforcing some of the skills learnt in class. Much of the popular literature is out of date (but see Midgley and Fox, 1986) but geography teachers can keep in touch with developments through appropriate channels and agencies.

Graphicacy

Some pupils with special needs and poor spatial intelligence may have almost as much difficulty producing and interpreting maps and sketches as they have with writing and reading. Others may be quite talented artists and should be encouraged to develop these skills through geography.

Ways of introducing map skills are tackled by Catling (1988) for the primary phase, and by Boardman (1986) for secondary schools. It should be remembered that five of the six mapping skills — scale, orientation, direction, grid references and altitude — are maths-based concepts and only one — symbols — is purely graphic. (The last is however of growing importance in road-warning signs, department store advisory notices and instructions for using appliances provided by manufacturers.) Again, topology — networks of road and railways — is crucial to both geography and mathematics (Folland, 1982)

One of my favourite methods of teaching mapwork is to relate a map with an aerial photograph, either vertical or oblique, of the same area — such the aerial view of London used as an introduction in the television series *Eastenders*. This technique should not be considered new, though it *is* the chief approach used in a series *New Ways in Geography* (Cole and Benyon, 1977). The method was however used over 100 years ago, long before the invention of aircraft! In a book *Elementary Geography* (dated 1890) children were provided with a large scale map and a 'ballroom-view' of a village, with one of the new railways included, and were instructed to measure distances between certain features, using the scale provided.

Aerial photographs are found throughout the packs of the very successful Schools Council project *Geography for the Young School Leaver* with many materials and ideas suitable for less able children. In each case they were accompanied by 'worm's eye' view, outline sketches (as overlays) or large-scale maps, and teachers were advised to produce similar resources of their local areas. A group of Manchester teachers produced a set of aerial photographs, with associated resources, of Manchester, which the LEA printed for general use (Proctor, 1974) and which proved excellent for pupils with special needs not only with developing skills but in understanding urban morphology (Harwood, 1988).

Photographs are found in all geography textbooks nowadays but they are commonly included to illustrate some of the text rather than as the focus of attention and work to develop children's graphic skills. Teachers of pupils with special needs have to revert to their own visual resources — slides or prints — to produce worksheets designed to develop skills. Textbook writers are increasingly using cartoons to show the views of people depicted in 'clouds' for teaching about, say, conflicting views of recreational use of national parks. These and other text books sketches are extremely valuable for use with pupils with special needs.

In my own teaching I have always tried to encourage pupils with special needs to draw the same sketches which the rest of the class are attempting. I adopt a slow step-by-step approach to build up a blackboard sketch, which they draw with continual help and prompting. Lightly drawn construction lines can help them to draw a fairly accurate sketch. But in many cases pupils with special needs will have to be presented with outline sketches which they complete or annotate. One example is a series of sketches to depict traditional operations of the Canadian timber industry, drawn by a former colleague, A.G. Halliday. The sketches demonstrate the value of graphicacy, for they tell a story which would otherwise require pages of text, and which can lead to diverse activities in class, including oral skills through discussion, role-playing and decision-making and class literacy, through creative writing or notes. The simplest form is merely to draw boxes around a sketch in which pupils with special needs annotate features while more able children can write more copious notes; this technique is illustrated elsewhere (Proctor, 1990a). One of the best ways to use the sketches of Canadian lumbering is to ask children to draw, on a double-page spread in their exercise books, a simple sketch-map of the river and its tributary, depicted in the sketches. The six sketches can then be cut up and glued on the sketch map, with arrows to the locations depicted — all neatly coloured, numbered and annotated — dependent on where they decide to locate their sketches. This type of work, emphasising quality of presentation, is in line with the National Curriculum geography report, to which we now turn our attention.

The Order for geography was published by the DES in March 1991. Although this replaces all the earlier documents, it is worth retaining the final report of the geography working party (June 1990) since this includes good examples of schemes of work such as a ten-hour programme for teaching the Amazon basin in key stage 3. It also includes five paragraphs (8.10-8.14) on geography for pupils with special needs. Although these provide essentially background information on the Warnock Report, statementing, assessment, the concept of disadvantage and disability, and the role of the new technologies in helping pupils with special needs to gain a full educational experience, they also present the argument that children with special needs should be given full access to the geography curriculum. In contrast, the earlier report was extremely factually-based — almost a 'mastermind' approach to the study of the world — and would appear to have been far from the needs of children with special educational needs. Indeed it set the subject back decades (see Proctor, 1990b).

In the National Curriculum Order for geography there are five attainment targets and three profile components:

AT1 Geographical skills	PC1 Skills
AT2 Knowledge and understanding of places	PC2 Places
AT3 Human geography) AT4 Human geography) AT5 Environmental geography)	PC3 People and environment

A sequence of area studies has been devised, starting off with studies of fairly small localities, leading on to the study of the home region, and finally, in key stage 3 and 4, to the study of countries and regions. The number of statements of attainment has been drastically reduced from earlier documents, and this could be considered helpful to teachers of children with special needs.

There are, however, three major problems compared with the reports prepared by the geography working parties. The Orders, it should be remembered, are written by civil servants under ministerial instructions, not by educationists, and this no doubt explains some extraordinary changes:

1. The earlier report included, within AT1, four skills dealing with maps and diagrams, fieldwork, the use of secondary sources, and enquiry skills. These have now been reduced to just two — the use of maps and fieldwork techniques — and this is likely to work against children with special needs, who would probably prefer assessment of a wider range of skills.

2. 'Values and attitudes', which has always been a key element of geographical education, have been removed. AT4 does not now include the more political and environmental issues, and reference to viewpoints and attitudes has been deleted from AT5. Many geographers feel that this interference by DES decimates their subject and makes it a less meaningful subject for all pupils.

3. In the programmes of study, the civil servants have re-written the statement 'Pupils should explain...' in the original proposal as 'Pupils should be taught...'. This shift of emphasis from learning activities to direct teaching is to be deplored, and may particularly hinder the development of geographical education for children with special needs.

The non-statutory guidance published by the National Curriculum Council (1991) provides useful suggestions for teachers. Without this guidance, the value of geography is developing children's skills, their curiosity and their outlook on life and other people would have been seriously reduced. The section of special educational needs is very short, but it does at least give an example (with reference to AT4, level 1a) of differentiating the curriculum for pupils with learning difficulties. The NCC promise more guidance, and it is to be hoped that this will more adequately address approaches to pupils with special needs in geography.

References

Balchin, W.G.V. and Coleman, A.M. (1965) 'Graphicacy should be the fourth ace in the pack', *Times Educational Supplement*, 5 November.

Barnes, D. (1976) *'From Communication to Curriculum'*, London: Penguin.

Boardman, D. (Ed.) (1986) *Handbook for Geography Teachers*, Sheffield: The Geographical Association.

Catling, S. (1988) 'Maps and mapping' In: Mills, D. (Ed.) *Geographical Work in Primary and Middle Schools*, Sheffield: The Geographical Association.

Cole, J.P. and Benyon, N.J. (1977) *New Ways in Geography*, Oxford: Blackwell.

Department of Education and Science (1975) *A Language for Life*, (The Bullock Report), London: HMSO.

Department of Education and Science (1978) *Special Educational Needs* (The Warnock Report), London: HMSO.

Department of Education and Science (1980) *A Framework for the School Curriculum*, London: HMSO.

Department of Education and Science (1982) *Mathematics Counts* (The Cockcroft Report), London: HMSO.

Department of Education and Science (1989) *National Curriculum: From Policy to Practice*, London: DES.

Earish, J. (1985) 'Drama and creative work', In: Corney, G. and Rawling, E. (Eds.) *Teaching Slow Learners Through Geography*, Sheffield: The Geographical Association.

Folland, M. (1982) 'Using road networks', In: Boardman, D. (Ed.) *Geography with Slow Learners*, Sheffield: The Geographical Association.

Gardner, H. (1984) *Frames of Mind: The Theory of Multiple Intelligences*, London: Heinemann.

Guilford, J.P. (1967) *The Nature of Human Intelligence*, London: McGraw-Hill.

Hartley, J. (1988) 'The typographical design of worksheets', In: Dilkes, J.L. and Nicholls, A. (Eds.) *Low Attainers and the Teaching of Geography*, Sheffield: The Geographical Association.

Harwood, D. (1988) Introducing mapwork to ESN(M) children through aerial photographs.

Hull, C. (1985) 'Drafting and authenticity in pupils' work', *Teaching Geography*, 10(3), pp.105-6.

Lewis, P.F. (1985) 'Beyond description', *Annals of the Association of American Geographers,* 75(4), pp.465-77.

Lorac, C. and Weiss, M. (1981) *Communication and Social Skills,* London: Wheaton.

Midgley, H. and Fox, P. (1988) 'Microcomputers in the classroom', In: Boardman, D. (Ed.) (1986) *Handbook for Geography Teachers,* Sheffield: The Geographical Association.

National Curriculum Council (1989) *The National Curriculum and Whole Curriculum Planning* (Circular No.6), York: NCC.

National Curriculum Council (1991) *Geography Non-Statutory Guidance,* York: NCC.

Paterson, J.H. (1979) 'Some dimensions of geography', *Geography,* 64(4), pp.268-78.

Proctor, N. (1974) 'Aerial photographs in geography teaching', *Teachers Talking,* December.

Proctor, N. (1985a) 'Educational Psychology and curriculum design: a child-centred approach', *Educational Studies,* 11(2), pp.151-8.

Proctor, N. (1985b) 'Redefining the basis of primary education', *Education 3-13,* 13(1), pp.5-8.

Proctor, N. (1985c) 'Marking and recording', *Teaching Geography,* 10(3), pp.103-4.

Proctor, N. (1987) 'Writing a special needs curriculum statement', *Education Today,* 37(2), pp.10-17.

Proctor, N. (Ed.) (1990a) *The Aims of Primary Education and the National Curriculum,* Basingstoke: Falmer Press.

Proctor, N. (199b) 'The good, the bad and the ugly: observations on the geography interim report', *Education, 23 March, pp.289-90.*

Renwick, M. (1981) 'Music and Songs', In: Boardman, D. *GYSL with Disadvantaged,* Sheffield: The Geographical Association.

Tansley, E. and Gulliford, R. (1960) *The Education of Slow- Learning Children,* London: Routledge and Kegan Paul.

Valletutti, P.J. et.al (Eds.) (1989) *Facilitating Communication in Young Children with Handicapping Conditions: A Guide for Special Education,* Boston: College Hill Press.

Wilson, M.D. (1981) *The Curriculum in Special Schools: Programme 4 — Individual Pupils,* London: Schools Council.

Chapter 8

Careers Education and Guidance for Pupils with Special Needs

Mary Greaves and Dorothy Sydenham

Introduction

It is important to emphasise that Career Officers do not work in isolation: they must co-operate fully with parents, teachers, tutors, employers and training providers. This is true for every aspect of their work and it is particularly important when pupils with special educational needs are considered. A consequence of this is that the reader may find some overlap with other chapters in this book.

The LEA Careers Service

In its present form the LEA Careers Service was set up in April 1974. Its statutory base is the Employment and Training Act, 1973, which made the provision of a careers service mandatory on all LEAs. Prior to that date the Careers Service's predecessor, the Youth Employment Service, was operated partly by LEAs and partly by the Department of Employment. Each LEA now has a duty to provide vocational guidance to pupils and students in their final years in full-time education and an employment service to those leaving education establishments. The provision of vocational guidance is the distinctive task of careers officers, and LEAs are obliged to appoint trained careers officers to carry out the work and also provide careers officers in places convenient for the public. LEAs may, if they wish, provide services

117

to adults and others to whom their statutory duty does not apply. Each LEA also decides how many careers officers and other staff to employ and determines their salary scales. There is no national salary scale for careers officers and there can be wide differences in the pay offered by different LEAs. This makes staff recruitment and retention a constant source of concern, not to say irritation, to Careers Service managers.

It is probably true to say that there are as many careers services as there are LEAs; each has its own distinct character and flavour. The great strength of the LEA Careers Service, like all other Local Authority services, is its ability to reflect local conditions and priorities.

Having said this, there are broad similarities between careers services. They all maintain close and regular contact with schools and colleges; pay great attention to the provision of up- to-date information about careers, further and higher education, employment and training opportunities; offer an impartial guidance service independent of individual educational institutions; seek to work closely with parents (the greatest single influence whether for good or ill on their children's career choices); keep in regular touch with employers and training providers to make sure the information they pass on is accurate and up-to-date, help employers and training providers fill vacancies, and offer an employment service to young people in their early years at work. In some areas information and guidance services are available to adults.

Careers officers place the welfare of the individual at the head of their professional work. They see their role as one of helping individual young people make their way through the transition — often a lengthy process — between school and work. The route may be a direct one but these days it is more likely to take in periods of training, either full or part-time possibly including time at college.

Pupils with special educational needs have always occupied a particular place in the work of careers officers and they have long been at the forefront of those advocating good training and further education provision for this group. Careers officers have had significant influence on government agencies and the development of programmes for young people with special needs within youth training owes much to their efforts.

Team work

The Careers Service has to work closely with the other agencies concerned with young people with special needs besides teachers and parents. School medical officers provide medical reports for the Careers Service. A Y9 is normally supplied for children with minor disabilities which may affect their suitability for some types of work. The form does not disclose medical information but indicates certain conditions that should be avoided in working environments. A Y10 is a more detailed report which discloses medical information and is used for more severely handicapped school leavers. The words 'more severely' give rise to grave concern on the part of parents especially. Y10s can be used as medical evidence for registering as a disabled person in some cases — a subject covered later in this chapter. However, there are no such forms to indicate social, emotional and behavioural difficulties.

Careers officers also work in conjunction with the Employment Medical Advisory Service once a young person enters the employment field. The Employment Medical Advisory Service comes under the Health and Safety Executive and gives advice to employers on the aspects of health and safety involved in recruiting people with disabilities.

Social workers, probation officers, medical advisors, occupational therapists and other professionals can all help a careers officer to build up a background in order to give relevant and effective advice to a special needs school leaver. Often the confines of confidentiality make written reports difficult but we are all here for the benefit of the client and such hurdles are usually successfully overcome. A careers officer dealing with young people who have special needs tries to consult the school medical officer, matron and nurse and, of course, parents. It is often necessary to talk to parents of handicapped pupils as early as the fourth year in order to explain the on-going options for their son or daughter once they reach 16 years of age. The majority of parents and disabled young people are unaware of the many provisions available both in education and employment. The realisation by parents that their child is approaching adulthood, and all the implications involved, causes increasing fears and worries which are all too easily, but unintentionally, passed on to the young person. To be able to allay those fears by giving information about local and national provision forms a much firmer basis for effective careers guidance. However, it is important that whenever possible the young person must be the one to make the decisions albeit with help, advice and guidance from parents, teachers, and careers officers.

Working in schools

In most careers services there is a careers officer who specialises in work with and for special needs school leavers and young people. Some local education authorities have recently introduced a policy whereby all careers officers work with the whole ability range of pupils and young people, including those who have special needs. Oxfordshire is one such authority and all careers officers within Oxfordshire Careers Service interview clients from the severely mentally handicapped to those graduating from universities. Prior to this the specialist career officer had to cover the more severely disabled school leavers, offering appropriate careers and vocational guidance coupled with realistic Further Education and training. The words 'more severely' caused problems, as no two people seem to have the same conception of what constitutes a 'severe' handicap. The problem of giving careers guidance to pupils termed as 'those having special needs of a more severe nature' in mainstream schools, was that such youngsters were seen by a different careers officer from the rest of their class, which singled them out from their peers. The new conception of careers guidance in Oxfordshire has at least overcome this problem.

The *Careers Service Manual*, which is a set of guidelines produced at regular intervals by the Department of Employment and is laid down for all Careers Services in the United Kingdom, describes a handicapped pupil as 'one for whom, as a result of some disability, provision is in a special school, in a special class within an ordinary school, or by special arrangements within a normal class. Where necessary, provision may be made elsewhere from a school — e.g. at home.'

The new policy adopted by the Oxfordshire LEA meant that the specialist careers officer became responsible for careers work for all pupils in mainstream schools but carrying a certain percentage caseload of special needs leavers. There are many arguments both 'for' and 'against' dispensing with the post of the Specialist Careers Officer dealing with special needs school leavers and young workers. Working in a generic way means being far less isolated from colleagues since everyone is doing the same work.

The main disadvantage of mainstream careers officers covering the more severely handicapped special needs leavers is the question of the amount of time needed to deal with the many additional aspects involved in giving meaningful and positive careers guidance. It is also a very emotive field, often involving political issues, and in such circumstances it is sometimes very difficult to maintain an impartial view.

The 1990s will be a period of the implementation of the Education Reform Act 1988, the expansion of the Technical and Vocational Education Initiative, the development of National Vocational Qualifications, the establishment of Training and Enterprise Councils and yet another change in Youth Training provision. Changes in the Careers Service are imminent, causing much speculation about our future role within schools and the community.

The question is raised as to who are the pupils with special needs and how are they to be identified by the Careers Service. As one headmaster of a large mainstream school remarked, 'Every pupil in my school has special needs of some sort!' Where pupils have been statemented, their needs have been identified, but there are those without statements who fall short of what will be expected of them once they leave school and start work. Careers officers now have to draw up an Individual Action Plan for these school leavers. This subject is covered more fully later in this chapter. But how do we identify those young people who need extra support in the working world? Lack of academic skills does not always result in lack of basic work or employment skills. Again, different people have varying conceptions of the definition of 'severe'. Assessment of academic ability is on-going and the national curriculum will hopefully increase the chances of special needs pupils following courses in more traditional basic subjects, albeit to a minor degree.

National Records of Vocational Achievement (NROVA), recently described by a lad with moderate learning difficulties as 'a cross between a scrapbook and a sort of diary in a box', contain written evidence of achievement intended to help motivate the less able towards higher goals. The Careers Service becomes involved in Key Stage 4 in the National Curriculum but at the time of writing the directions for careers guidance in education have not been published, making it difficult to go more deeply into the effect upon special needs pupils. It is impossible to take any part of the learning process in isolation, and careers guidance is as important to a school leaver with severe learning difficulties as to the 'A' level leaver who happens to be in a wheelchair.

The Careers Service relies on staff in schools and education department administration to identify potential leavers who may have difficulties seeking, obtaining or keeping employment. Some school leavers may never reach a level of employability by normal standards. In the case of those needing special care the future is considered under the Disabled Persons (Services, Consultation & Representation) Act 1986, but for many sixteen-year-olds with less obvious problems, the four years after statutory school leaving age are vital. The groundwork is implemented in schools but some problems emerge after leaving the school environment. Young people who have special educational needs may be able to offer manual and practical basic working skills upon which to build some expertise, although very often their short concentration span presents problems to an employer. However, for some young people having to leave the security of the school environment creates social and emotional pressures that could not have been envisaged previously.

The Transition from School to Work

Because the term 'special needs' embraces all the fields of handicap, the employment prospects and academic levels of these schools leavers are varied. For those of average intelligence and above, quite a few will progress through further and higher education, and the advent of the National Curriculum should present few problems since timing of attainment of the goals is not the main issue, only the achievement. Thus, the fact that many impaired pupils are a year behind their peers should be less problematical in the future. One of the main difficulties facing careers officers is that sometimes these youngsters, who are eligible to leave at statutory school leaving age, decide during the school holidays to return to school, despite perhaps having led school staff to believe otherwise. When schools are closed it is difficult to obtain background information if the careers officer has not seen the young person, not to mention the difficulty for the youngster who may have had little, or even no careers education in the third and fourth years. It is fair to say that sometimes it is the pressure put on the young person at home by the family circumstances, especially where an extra weekly wage packet may make a considerable difference to the quality of life for the family, that determines whether a student should leave school. For the 'just par' there is every chance that with a little support, perhaps on a Youth Training programme that caters for special needs trainees, they will obtain employment eventually. But for the severely handicapped, especially the severely mentally handicapped and those needing special care, it is reasonable to assume they will not be able to compete with other workers in the open employment field and will need sheltered employment or special care. But what of the 'in betweens'? These are the youngsters who often need a great deal of help and advice, especially if they have little or no family backing, but who are not entitled to register as disabled for employment purposes. These young people have to take their chances of survival within open employment. Many of these young people have personality defects and/or behavioural problems which preclude them from being able to fit in with the existing workforce, or their behaviour is such that employers have to dispense with their services rather than have their disruptive influence within the workplace.

Employment Opportunities for Leavers with Special Needs

a. The employment field

A careers officer has to work with employers and have an understanding of local and national employment requirements in order to be able to submit young people under the Placement Service for people in their early years at work which the Careers Service administers. This involves having an in-depth knowledge of local and national employers' expectations and demands.

With constant changes in examination procedures and subject titles, it is not surprising that employers have difficulty in understanding some of the terminology and content of courses. Purely academic subjects such as the core subjects of the National Curriculum are more easily understood and allied to modules within training for employment. Here again it is hoped that the National Vocational Qualifications will assist in more uniform levels of assessment and measurement of goals. Whether young people with special needs will have the same opportunities as their more able colleagues remains to be seen.

Where school leavers have been in residential schools out of their home county, careers officers liaise with each other. The careers office in whose area the school is situated has the responsibility for giving careers guidance there and the client is usually invited to attend the local careers office during holidays to discuss local further education, higher education, training or employment opportunities. In this respect National Vocational Qualifications should eventually clarify some of the confusion caused by the proliferation of certificates and diplomas no matter in which part of the country the applicant acquired his or her education or training. The Careers Service endeavours to impart relevant and meaningful information to all leavers from full-time education. In 1992 we will also have to extend our expertise to cover opportunities within the European Economic Community.

b. Interpretation of 'disability'

The severity of a disability largely depends on several factors especially the amount of handicap it directly inflicts, the attitude of the person who has the disability and the attitude of other people, and the personality and the environment of the disabled person.

The 1988 Education Reform Act incorporates the phrase 'special needs', not the words 'handicap', 'disability' or 'impairment'. The variety of implications associated with particular handicaps upon the young person's learning ability are open to broad interpretation. For employment purposes such disabilities must be more clearly defined. The following is the more usual terminology when assessing for employment:

IMPAIRMENT	denotes defective organ or function
DISABILITY	denotes what cannot be done
HANDICAP	denotes lack of ability to do the job in question

A proportion of the unstatemented pupils with special needs will join the open labour market and have to compete in later life with their peers, for whom the National Curriculum has much clearer goals and preparation value. Of the remaining pupils some will go into less demanding employment, some may manage sheltered employment, and a few will be unable to undertake any form of paid work. More especially, in the case of the latter, learning- for-life features in their curriculum from a fairly early age, but from the age of 14 it plays a very significant part in preparing the young person for adulthood. It is essential for teenagers with special needs to be given every opportunity to develop socially, since they are usually much more immature than their peers. This is where the non-statutory guidelines concerning cross-curriculum activities in the National Curriculum assume special importance.

In this respect the Technical and Vocational Education Initiative (TVEI) is having a noticeable impact on careers education in schools, both mainstream and special. Unfortunately, many employers are experiencing difficulties, mainly because high interest rates and the new Business Rate, in addition to the Poll Tax, has left many small firms struggling for financial survival. With so much demand for work experience places, some areas of the country will be hard put to come up with sufficient placements to satisfy the demand, especially in rural areas and non-industrial districts. School leavers with special needs, with or without statements, will undoubtedly be nearer the bottom of the queue for work experience placements. It is important that these youngsters have a chance of as much realistic work experience as possible: helping in the school kitchen, running errands for the school secretary, helping the caretaker or the groundsman, is all good basic experience and should be encouraged, but it should be additional to, not instead of, work experience outside school.

c. Types of employment available

There are several types of employment available — open, sheltered, home, self, full-time, part-time, and voluntary.

Open employment is the general employment field in competition with the rest of the workforce. *Sheltered* employment is that which takes into account the restrictions of a disabled person. It is not always possible to make an accurate prognosis during school life as to the level of employment at which a special needs leaver will ultimately function. For this reason extended education courses, bridging courses, and similar 'stepping stones' are invaluable prior to Youth Training or employment.

There are various interest guides and assessment exercises which can be used with lower ability pupils and students and some fairly sophisticated computerised assessment modules are now on the market.

The Disabled Persons Register (Registration under the Disabled Persons (Employment) Act 1944 and 1958) is a voluntary register of people with disabilities which is kept by the Employment Service. Under this Act a Disabled Person is 'one who, on account of injury, disease or congenital deformity, is substantially handicapped in obtaining or keeping employment, or in undertaking work on his or her own account, of a kind which, apart from that injury, disease or deformity, would be suited to his or her age, experience and qualifications'. Learning difficulties of a moderate level are not included in this definition as the handicap is based on educational criteria and is not, for the purposes of the Act, an employment problem. Eligibility for inclusion in the register is dependent upon certain conditions, including the disabled person having the wish to work and a 'reasonable prospect' of obtaining and keeping some form of employment. The decision to go on the register is purely a voluntary one and is effected through the Disablement Resettlement Office often via the careers officer. School children below the statutory school leaving age are not eligible for registration.

There are clear advantages in registration. For example, every employer with twenty or more workers must employ a certain proportion of registered disabled people (currently three per cent). This is the Quota System, often referred to as the Green Card System. Another advantage is that severely disabled people who are registered can also be given help in various ways under the special schemes for disabled persons. Vacancies for car park attendants and passenger electric lift attendants are reserved for registered disabled people.

d. Special schemes for the disabled

The most significant of the schemes as far as young people are concerned is the *Sheltered Placement Scheme* which provides integrated job opportunities for severely disabled people in open employment and offers a wide variety of jobs in different industries and occupations at all ability levels. Sheltered Placement Schemes involve a sponsor which employs the person and a host company which provides the work. The sponsor and the host have a contract whereby the disabled person's services are made available to the host and for which the host pays an agreed wage based on the disabled person's percentage of 'normal' output. In Oxfordshire this scheme has been extremely successful in placing both mentally and physically young people in employment after Youth Training.

Under the *Adaptation to Premises and Equipment Scheme* grants may be paid to employers who make essential adaptations to equipment or premises to enable an employee with disabilities to undertake employment.

The Assistance with Fares to Work Scheme is designed to assist certain disabled people to meet the cost of their fares to and from work.

Special Aids to Employment Scheme enables people with disabilities to keep a job by issuing equipment or tools free on permanent loan.

These are only some of the special measures available to disabled workers, but it must be stressed that in order to take advantage of any scheme the person must be capable of doing the job. Other help available through voluntary organisations include *The Pathway Employment Service,* whereby Mencap offer employers financial incentive and a gratuity to a fellow worker throughout the training of a mentally handicapped person, and the *Personal Readers Service* through the Royal National Institute for the Blind, which provides financial assistance to take on a part-time reader for a blind or partially sighted employee.

Youth Training and Individual Action Plans

As from May 1990 the Careers Service became involved in the drawing up of Individual Action Plans. At present these have to be issued for all school leavers who may have difficulty reaching NVQ level 1. The plan is drawn up by the young person and a careers officer, and states the present position before going on the describe the career goals they have in mind and the learning, training or other experiences needed to reach these. It then sets out the different routes to reach the preferred goals using education, training and work, and finishes with what the young person and the careers officer can do to help the client achieve the goals. Individual Action Plans can be updated and should be reviewed every three months. Individual Action Plans are drawn up before the client leaves school and should be the path envisaged by the young person with help and guidelines from the careers officer. It must be in language the young person can understand. There are actually three categories in the Special Training need Category for Youth Training which are defined as follows in the Guidelines issued to careers officers:

> *Category A* Young people whose disadvantages initially prevent access to vocational training and who require a period of Initial Training and preparation. This period must be specified at no more than six months, and provision must comply the Initial Training Design Framework.

> *Category B* Young people for whom Training aimed at NVQ level 2 is not thought to be realistic on the basis of current assessment. All such young people must be offered Independent Action Plans and must be given the help and support they need to progress as far as they can towards general and vocational competence.

> *Category 3* Young people who have some prospect of achieving NVQ level 2 but in order to do so need significant additional support and longer duration of Training. All these categories are linked to a Special Training Needs Code of Practice.

It is therefore important that young people with special needs who are capable of employment, whether statemented or not, are given the opportunity both at school and during Youth Training, to fulfil their potential initially within the National Curriculum and later in life through a National Vocational Qualification.

Certain Youth Training courses provide 'taster' type courses including work on employers' premises, which are designed especially for those youngsters who need both the extra support and an individual programme. These are mostly those individuals for whom the careers officer has drawn up an Individual Action Plan, and the course providers are given a small amount of extra funding to cover the extra work involved, provided the young people concerned have been endorsed by a careers officer. It has to be said that there are many special needs young people who have successfully completed Youth Training without such a support and some have been on employer-based programmes.

In addition to Local Training the Employment Rehabilitation Service provides two other types of provision. Assessment Courses lasting between 2-13 weeks are designed to assess the most suitable two year Youth Training course for individual young people. The content of such a course is flexible and is aimed at meeting that young person's needs and also the needs of the locality. The other provision is off-the-job training which is designed to meet individual needs and forms an integral part of a Youth Training placement.

There are also two types of courses at Employment Rehabilitation Centres for which young people who are not eligible for Youth Training may apply.

These are Short Assessment Courses and Rehabilitation Courses which often involve the necessity of living away from home for a short period.

There is a Disablement Resettlement Officer (DRO) in each area who helps to find work and training for disabled people under the Government's Special Measures Schemes (other than Youth Training). Career officers who are dealing with special needs school leavers and young people keep in regular touch with the local Employment Services staff and DRO's who are based in Employment Services Centres (formerly known as Job Centres).

Disablement Advisory Service teams are small teams of staff who assist employers in policies and practices of recruiting disabled workers and also advise disabled people with individual problems to help them succeed in their employment.

Conclusion

With such a variety of schemes and resources available to help with employment of the disabled, it is to be hoped the National Curriculum will eventually be adapted to lay the foundations for ensuring that every schoolchild with special needs, whether severely or moderately affected, will have the best possible chance to develop academic, work and life skills, so that they can have a chance to join the world or work in whatever capacity suitable to their situation.

When considering all the options and decisions confronting school leavers, it is essential to remember that in the case of special needs leavers we are trying to provide equal opportunities in line with those afforded to their peers. We try to give them positive aims and motivation to overcome failure. One of the objectives must be to help special needs youngsters take their place in society with self-respect and esteem.

As the introduction of local management of school (LMS) league tables and open enrolment impose a necessity for schools to obtain good examination results in order to increase their attraction to parents, it is feared that pupils with special needs, who may well not be high achievers and most certainly need extra financial resources, are unlikely to be the most sought-after additions to school rolls. It is hoped that this will not happen, and as the national curriculum becomes established, perhaps the position of pupils with special needs will be reviewed in the light of experience. Defined relevant cross-curricular themes will need to be developed to enable them to participate fully in school activities.

A certainty at present is that education and training is being subjected to a period of massive change and upheaval. Pressures are being placed on schools and colleges as a consequence of the arrangements for local financial management. Current demographic changes and the decline in the numbers of young people eligible to leave school are creating recruitment difficulties for employers, though some may be balanced by rising unemployment. Furthermore, falling school rolls, together with the dawning recognition of the relative lack of training and further education for young people in the United Kingdom compared with its international competitors, are combining to place even greater pressure than hitherto on young people to remain longer within the educational system. The newly created Training and Enterprise Councils are very largely an unknown factor at present but they could well have a significant effect on local training opportunities. Even the Careers Service could find itself working in a different environment once the results of an internal review being carried out by the Department of Employment is made public.

Whatever the outcome of all this, there can be no denying the need for all young people, whatever their abilities, to have the right of access to independent, accurate and up-to-date information and guidance as they approach the time to make crucial choices affecting their futures. The Careers Service, regardless of which body has responsibility for its operation, will continue to be uniquely placed to play a full part in this task.

NB. The opinions and views expressed in this chapter are those of the authors: they do not necessarily represent those of their current or previous employers.

Chapter 9

Assessing Achievement in the National Curriculum: Reporting Failure or Recording Success?

Barry Stierer

Introduction

Assessment is arguably the cornerstone of the 1988 Education Reform Act. Legislation inspired by a determination to inject the values of the market-place into the education service requires *information* about the performance of pupils, teachers and schools in order to enable, at least, the appearance of 'informed' comparison by parents, policy-makers and the holders of purse-strings. The assessment apparatus (or 'arrangements', to use the official discourse of understatement) therefore needs to be understood in the broad context of the Act in all its provisions, and not merely as an adjunct to the National Curriculum. Information derived from assessment procedures will be used not only by practitioners when evaluating and planning curriculum and teaching, but possibly also by parents when choosing a school for their children and by local education authorities when calculating individual schools' devolved budgets. Assessment in this sense is inseparable from policies such as open enrolment and local management of schools.

There is understandable anxiety about the impact that these procedures for assessment will have on schools, teachers, pupils and their parents. It is the objective of this chapter to examine how assessment arrangements within the National Curriculum are affecting work with pupils with special educational needs, and to discuss the changes which those arrangements will bring about, as well as ways in which good practice may survive.

A few explanatory remarks may be needed. First, I shall use the term 'pupils with special education needs' in a broad sense, to mean 'low attaining pupils'. I will certainly not confine myself to children in special education institutions, or those with 'statements' of special education need, or even necessarily the 20% of pupils which the Warnock Report identified as likely to require special help at some time in their school careers. Second, although special attention must be given to the implications for the educational provision for pupils with special educational needs, these are in many cases identical to the implications for pupils of *all* needs and abilities.

Third, the shape of the assessment system within the national curriculum was, at the time of writing, not known in precise detail. Decisions were still to be made on a number of crucial issues such as reporting results of assessment, standard assessment tasks (SATs), teacher assessment (TA), aggregation, moderation and so on. It was only possible in this chapter to discuss the assessment arrangements at a particular point in their evolution.

The system for national assessment

The framework for the system of national assessment was devised by the Task Group on Assessment and Testing (TGAT) chaired by Professor Paul Black. TGAT reported in January 1988 (DES, 1988a) and their recommendations were broadly accepted by the Secretary of State in June 1988 (DES, 1988b). Although the system envisaged by TGAT has been modified through a series of re-interpretations by National Curriculum subject working groups and through various attempts at 'clarification' by the National Curriculum Council (NCC), the School Examinations and Assessment Council (SEAC) and the Department of Education and Science (DES), the general framework proposed by TGAT remains intact. The main features of that framework are:

a. Each of the ten 'foundation' subjects (including the three 'core' subjects of English, Mathematics and Science) are divided into a small number of Profile Components (PCs), and each Profile Component is further divided into a number of Attainment Targets (ATs). PCs and ATs are very general aspects of the curriculum, and are expressed independently of age or level of attainment.

b. Pupils' attainment within these parts of the curriculum are expressed using numerical levels on a ten-level scale, with Level 1 being the lowest and Level 10 the highest. TGAT conceptualised Levels as very substantial increments in a pupil's learning, each representing about two years of 'educational growth'.

c. Within each Attainment Target, one or more Statements of Attainment (SOAs) will be devised to describe learning within that part of the curriculum at *each* of the ten levels. These Statements will describe in positive terms what a child knows, understands and is able to do at each of the Levels. Moreover, TGAT envisaged that the Statements would reflect a principle of progression within the curriculum and not be related to 'average' performance at specified ages.

d. TGAT envisaged a system for national assessment which was criterion-referenced, as opposed to norm-referenced, as described in the preceding paragraph. However, they also 'speculated' (but with no empirical evidence in support) that 'average' seven-year-olds would perform at around Level 2, average eleven- year-olds at Level 4, average 14-year-olds between Levels 5 and 6, and average 16-year-olds between Levels 6 and 7. By speculating thus, the Task Group gave a strong steer to the subject working groups devising Statements of Attainment for each subject, and ensured that most people within and outside the education service understand the national assessment system to be essentially age-related.

e. Formal assessment and reporting would happen at the end of four Key Stages, i.e. at around the ages of 7,11, 14 and 16. Formal assessment would consist of judgements made by teachers ('Teacher Assessment' or 'TA'), combined with results for externally-developed assessment materials ('Standard Assessment Tasks' or 'SATs'). Individual pupils' results would be reported to their parents, and results would be aggregated to enable the publication of school results on an annual basis.

It is worth noting briefly some of the more significant modifications and official interpretations which have been made to the TGAT framework in the two years or so since its publication:

a. In June 1988, the Secretary of State broadly accepted the framework proposed by TGAT, with one or two notable qualifications. For example, whereas TGAT recommended that 'there should be no requirement to publish results for pupils at age 7' (DES, 1988a para 137), the Secretary of State stated that 'it is strongly recommended that schools should do so' — that is, to publish aggregated school results at the end of Key Stage 1 (DES, 1988b).

b. In July 1989 (DES, 1989), SEAC advised the Secretary of State that, in the event of discrepancies between the results of Teacher Assessment and the results of SATs, the SAT result should be 'preferred', This is unlikely to arise frequently, but the Secretary of State's acceptance of SEAC's advice disappointed many professionals who felt that teachers' judgements, based on the collection of evidence and close observation of pupils over a sustained period of schooling, should be given *at least* parity with assessments carried out over a relatively short period of time in a stylised context.

c.   Many of the Statements of Attainment devised by subject working groups appeared to be inconsistent with the principle of progression, with remarkably uneven 'gaps' between the levels. Moreover, there appeared to be no apparent consistency in the degree of difficulty inherent in Statements within different subjects at the same Levels.

d.   Whilst TGAT envisaged a system within which Levels would be assigned *retrospectively* at the end of Key Stages, much of the support material produced has suggested that Statements of Attainment are capable of being used far more frequently as a tool for regular recording of progress.

e.   GCSE will be the main form of certification in all subjects at the end of Key Stage 4 (i.e. at 16+). However, the signs are that a 'dual-track' system will be operated, with a less comprehensive 'National Curriculum' course running in parallel to GCSE for pupils who either do not opt to study a particular subject of GCSE standard or (most relevant for the purposes of this chapter) who are unlikely to attain higher than Level 4 in a subject at 16+.

f.   The number of attainment targets and scope of learning to be formally assessed has been drastically reduced.

Formative assessment and summative assessment

A good deal of the anxiety experienced by practitioners over assessment within the National Curriculum stems, in my view, from a widespread tendency at all levels of the system to conflate what I see as two distinct stages of assessment — formative and summative. Most of the new assessment procedures emanating from the 1988 Education Reform Act fall into the category of summative assessment, whereas most of the everyday assessment practices used by teachers are essentially formative. The purpose of this section is to argue that good habits of formative assessment will not only be possible within the new arrangements, but should be positively encouraged in order to safeguard the centrality of the teacher-pupil relationship and to ensure that summative assessment will be validly rooted in the processes of teaching and learning.

Summative assessment is best understood as a stock-taking exercise carried out at regular, but relatively infrequent, intervals. It is a process of portraying, retrospectively, progress that has been achieved since the preceding stock-take. It is an attempt by a teacher to recognise the patterns in a child's learning which have emerged over a sustained period. Summative assessment often has a public dimension: It may culminate in a report to parents, or to teachers in the same or another school, or to other professionals. In this sense, summative assessment comprises considered judgements relating to the point an individual child has reached, addressed to a public audience. The language in which the outcomes of summative assessment are expressed must therefore be intelligible to a wide range of potential 'users'.

Within the framework for National Curriculum assessment, Statements of Attainment are the criteria against which summative assessment of pupils will be conducted at the end of Key Stages, through some combination of Standard Assessment Tasks (SATs) and teachers' assessment (TA). Although the Statements of Attainment unquestionably represent only a narrow range of achievement, and although many of the Statements are hopelessly ambiguous, they are nevertheless best understood as the paraphernalia of summative assessment. Whilst this point may appear to be self-evident, it needs to be clearly made, because in the short time Statements of Attainment have been with us they have been widely misused and misrepresented. Many of the bodies responsible for disseminating information and providing guidance to teachers on the subject of National Curriculum assessment have, deliberately or otherwise, promoted the notion that Statements of Attainment can function both formatively as well as summatively. This notion needs to be soundly refuted — perhaps especially in relation to pupils with special educational needs.

We need to recall that Statements of Attainment are not merely a series of progressive steps which different children move through at different rates. They represent an attempt, by the National Curriculum subject working groups, to *operationalise the ten levels* for a particular subject area. They are not therefore merely criteria; they are *level-specific criteria*. This means that they cannot be considered separately from the levels they represent.

What, then, *are* these levels? If, as TGAT proposed, levels represent two years of educational growth for an average child within attainment targets, they are *astronomical* increments of progress. We may expect many average children to take three or even four years to move from one level to the next within some attainment targets. If, on this reckoning, teachers stand in the classroom with a clipboard waiting for children to pass through a level, they will be waiting for a very long time. Indeed, even when children do pass through a level, there will be not flash of blue light, no clap of thunder. Levels, then, are not real and measurable things in the real world, like shoe sizes. They are (rather crude) ways of describing the *outcome* of summative assessment, retrospectively, at the end of a sustained period of schooling. Levels of attainment therefore relate to a time scale which is significantly different from the time scale within which teachers and pupils work in the classroom.

Such misunderstanding is partly attributable to the fact the the roots of TGAT's framework lie in the tradition of 'graded assessment'. Within graded assessment schemes, detailed criteria are established for finely-graded steps in learning. Children move through such assessment schemes at their own pace, and usually decide for themselves when to attempt to satisfy the criteria a the next step. The five years or so leading up to the TGAT report were characterised by the rapid development of graded assessment schemes, particularly in mathematics, science and modern languages. Indeed Professor Paul Black, who chaired TGAT, was an influential proponent of graded assessment. It is unfortunate that the framework devised by TGAT has many of the outward features of a graded assessment scheme, but is translated onto at time scale which, as I have said, differs radically from the one operating in the classroom.

It is difficult to imagine, therefore, how levels of attainment — and the Statement of Attainment which express them for each subject — can be used for the purposes of formative assessment. Nevertheless, a plethora of recording grids based on levels and statements of attainment are already in use in schools, which many teachers are using as frequently as once a week to record the levels individual children have reached. Whilst this misuse of levels and statements of attainment is distressing enough in relation to children making reasonable progress in their learning, it is especially distressing in the case of low-attaining pupils. If levels and statements of attainment are used as the 'unit of measurement' for routine recording it is inevitable that a significant proportion of children will appear to be making no progress whatever.

Formative assessment, on the other hand, is a continuous process of observing, recording and discussing children's learning and development in a way which is integral to everyday classroom activity. It is the *gradual* building up of a picture, and in this sense is more in step with the time scale at which teaching and learning take place. Formative assessment, if it becomes genuinely embedded in teachers' routine practice, can enhance the quality of children's learning and can, moreover, serve as a foundation for the more intermittent exercise of summative 'stock-taking' — a foundation which is soundly rooted in evidence arising from children's learning and which will therefore make the task of summative assessment more valid and less onerous than if it were carried out 'cold'.

What are the main features of formative assessment? First, it involves the routine collection of evidence arising from children's learning. We have for too long been wedded to a narrow conception of what constitutes evidence of children's learning and achievement. Written work represents only a small proportion of the potential range of evidence that might be collected, and it is vital — perhaps especially when working with low- attaining pupils — that we broaden our notion of what a comprehensive collection of evidence might comprise. Two-dimensional graphic and artistic work may be stored, and three-dimensional constructions may be photographed and then retained for future reference. Plans and designs, however rough, often provide more insight into the process of a child's learning than does the final product. Children's talk may occasionally be tape-recorded and transcribed. These various forms of evidence can be collected on a regular basis to create a cumulative *portfolio* of work which can contribute to children's sense of accomplishment as well as illustrate the pattern of a child's learning for assessment purposes.

However important it may be to consider the widest possible range of tangible evidence, much of a child's learning will not produce material outcomes which can be stored and subsequently retrieved. This may be especially true in the case of low-attaining pupils, whose learning is often an intangible process and whose small but significant steps will not manifest themselves in a material form. It is here that the teacher's skills of careful observation and descriptive recording are indispensable. Most of our associations with record-keeping militate against this kind of routine descriptive recording of observation. We tend to be reluctant to make an entry in a record book unless it has the appearance of a rounded and considered judgement about a child. This reluctance stems in large measure from understandable anxieties about the judgement which some third party might make about the intelligibility or accuracy of such entries. Grades, and ticks in boxes, may to some extent deflect such criticism, but they are incapable of portraying the immediacy of the process of children's learning. No single entry, or piece of evidence, will every capture the totality of a child's progress, or even the critical moment of real change. Entries in a teacher's 'jotter' should therefore be short fragments of narrative, which describe the detail of a child's observed activity in a way which is rooted in a specific time and place, and which are addressed essentially to no-one but the teacher concerned for her or his later reference. Frequently but briefly made, such fragmentary entries will gradually build up a picture which will enable a valid retrospective portrayal of the summative stock-taking point.

Another important source of evidence is of course pupils themselves. 'Assessment' has tended in the past to be something which 'happened to' pupils; this has in turn contributed significantly to the more general *passivity* which has characterised especially low-attaining pupils' relationship with their schooling. Evidence from the national evaluation of records of achievement pilot schemes (Broadfoot *et.al.,* 1988) suggests that involving pupils directly in the process of formative assessment helps to make the business of education more intelligible to them, which in turn enhances their sense of ownership and active control. Pupils can, for example, take an instrumental part in selecting evidence to be included in a portfolio of work. They can be helped to set short-term targets for themselves, and to review progress in relation to those targets at regular intervals.

Discussions with children are sometimes the most valid way of gaining access to the quality of those aspects of their learning which do not generate tangible outcomes. For example, talking to children about the stories, books, comics and articles they have read and listened to often provides more insight into their experiences of reading and listening then any other mode. such conversations can, in turn, be described in the kind of recording jotter described above. Pupils also often enjoy keeping diaries or logs which record their responses to books and stories, or more general reflections on their learning; these personal accounts may also contribute to their portfolios. Involving pupils in the process of formative assessment therefore serves a three-fold purpose: it enhances their motivation and skills of self-assessment; it provides insight into the process of learning, which can inform a day-to-day teaching; and it generates another body of evidence in an accumulating record of achievement.

Clearly, these essential features of formative assessment (collecting a wide range of evidence, recording everyday observations, and involving pupils) cannot simply be *imported* into a classroom. The notion of formative assessment I have developed here carries with it profound implications for teaching styles, classroom management and the organisation of learning. Regular discussions with pupils, and regular recording of observations, are simply impracticable if classroom practice is characterised predominantly by teacher-led activity. Time for formative assessment cannot be *won* from teaching time; practical ways must be developed which enable formative assessment to become a natural and integral part of everyday teaching. Classroom practice driven by formative assessment will involve sensitively supported group work and independent learning, and a willingness to relinquish our sense of indispensability in order to stand back, reflect, observe and record.

To summarise, I have advocated a child-centred and process-orientated model for formative assessment as the essential foundation for national assessment, for a number of reasons:

— Collecting evidence and recording observations enables a picture of a child's learning to build up gradually over time. These processes are much closer to the time scale at which teaching and learning take place than are the level-specific Statement of Attainment.

— Collecting evidence and recording observations on a continuous basis will make the task of summative assessment at the end of key stages a relatively straightforward task of 'retrospective portrayal', rather than special activity.

— Formative assessment feeds directly into teaching for individual children in a way which summative assessment cannot.

— Portfolios of evidence and records of observation can provide a focus for discussions with parents on a routine basis.

— Formative assessment involves pupils in their own learning.

— Formative assessment provides the evidence which will enable teachers to justify their judgements at the summative assessment stage.

— Formative assessment places due emphasis on the teacher's role in the assessment process, rather than that of external testing agencies.

Issues relating to pupils with special educational needs

However fully the distinction between summative and formative assessment is understood, and however fully the principles of formative assessment take root in everyday classroom practice, there remain a number of crucial issues arising from the national assessment arrangements which are of particular relevance and importance for teachers of pupils with special educational needs.

Aggregated school results

Under the 1988 Education Reform Act, schools will be required *by law* to publish aggregated results by subject, for pupils at the end of Key Stages 2, 3 and 4 (i.e. at ages 11, 14 and 16), and will be 'strongly encouraged' (DES, 1988b) to do so for pupils at the end of Key Stage 1 (i.e. at age 7). Schools will be expected to publish such results alongside 'a general report for the area, prepared by the local authority, to indicate the nature of socio-economic and other influences which are known to affect schools' (DES, 1988a). They will not however be permitted to *adjust* their results in order to compensate for the effect which certain intake variables might have. In this way, schools' results will be comparable in absolute terms rather than in terms of the 'educational value' which they had 'added' to their pupils. Viewed in the context of the 1988 Act as a whole, it is clear that there will be powerful incentives for schools to disapply pupils with special needs from the summative assessment procedures at the end of Key Stages. With the size of schools' delegated budgets now directly linked to the number of pupils on roll, and the size of schools' rolls inevitably dependent upon their ability to attract and sustain parental confidence, any scope for artificially 'massaging' the school's results by disapplying pupils with special needs will be understandably exploited. This, coupled with the practice in any LEAs of weighting pupils with special needs more heavily than other pupils in their LMS funding formulae, may spark an irresponsible rash of requests for statementing.

Should national assessment replace existing assessment procedures for pupils with special needs?

As I have argued above, national assessment, by which I mean the application of Statements of Attainment to children at the end of Key Stages using a combination of Standard Assessment Tasks (SATs) and teachers' assessments (TA), is essentially summative. It is not therefore capable of providing the kind of detailed diagnostic information about individual pupils which can inform decisions about meeting children's special educational needs —

either on an everyday basis in the classroom, or
of drawing up a statement of special educational
special teaching. The unsuitability of national ass
derives from three features of its underlying c
assessment is based upon a time scale which is i
assessment, as described above. Second, as Pat 7
tively shown, the national assessment system
principles of 'mastery learning', rather than c
Wedell *et.al* (1987) have emphasised, invalidat
ment for *any* pupil, but perhaps especially thos
needs. Third, the national assessment system ex
well as pupils from the process of assessment w
pointed out, threatens to undermine the gains th
the last decade in promoting collaborative asse
integrate parents and which are conducted on a n

In view of this mis-match between the purpose
for pupils with special educational needs and
assessment, it is clear that the claims made for
all-purpose system have been misguided or unr
example, that the system for national assessm
flexible to 'provide information which will help i
and weaknesses' (DES, 1988a, para 27) now see
School Examinations and Assessment Counci
claimed that national assessment will obviate to
existing procedures for diagnostic assessment:

> ...the assessment process of the National
> some degree provide information for screen
> partly by revealing profiles and performa
> targets, and partly by focusing on the ext
> them. (SEAC, 1989)

Given the severe limitations of the information
will provide, SEAC's statement seems more
thinking than of informed prediction.

To its credit, TGAT recognised the limited d
tional assessment would have, and recommendec
the chosen test development agency' be estab
producing 'a wide range of diagnostic tests', speci
the detailed information which national assessn
provide. They envisaged, for example, that a L
seven should automatically signal that the child r
that further materials should be available in ord
signal with fine-grain diagnostic investigation:

In the process of giving pupils with s.e.n. the
strate their level on the statements of attainme
find it necessary to structure their schemes of
to provide a series of intermediate goals, thoug
some attainment targets can be broken down n
into smaller steps. In such circumstances teach
their existing recording systems to bring them i
statements of attainment themselves but with t
to them. (SEAC, 1989).

The first point which must be made, in relation to tl
the national assessment system, is how lamentable i
achievable intervening targets has not been more wic
tion to *all* pupils. To use Statements of Attainment,
TGAT scale which they implicitly represent, as cr
assessment and recording, is not unlike using a metr
daily growth of beanplants. Due to a lack of clarity fro
agencies, teachers are labouring under the misconcept
Attainment represent the criteria against which they s
intervals of time for which the Statements were ne
already observed teachers using the Statements of A
basis and, in not-so-rare cases, in relation to individual
misuses of the Statements of Attainment prevent te
access to the day-to-day quality of children's learning
for *all* pupils realistic and understandable targets for v

The fact is, as Barrs *et.al.* (1990) have poignantly sa
no way, in terms of the National Curriculum, of recog
significant steps forward' (p.44). Accordingly, they rec
adopt methods of formative assessment such as the ILE
Record, which incorporates the principles of collecting
observations and involving pupils which were des
article.

Records of achievement

A great deal of development work has taken place ov
or so in the area of records of achievement. Comme
ations of that work are widely available (e.g. Broadfoo
foot *et.al.*, (1991), and there is therefore no need to
Nevertheless, no discussion of the assessment impl
Education Reform Act for pupils with special educati
complete without a brief reminder of the ways in whic
ment hold the potential for reconciling the importance c
educational needs of pupils with the demands of the A

By 'records of achievement' I intend a broad defini
a wide range of elements:

a. A range of documents developed for the purposes of recording and reporting pupils' achievements (both summative and formative);

b. Specific processes and activities which have been developed to enable the recording of achievement, such as teacher-pupil discussions, target-setting and review, pupil-assessment, the preparation of pupil statements and so on; and

c. A set of principles which can be applied to all teaching and learning, such as 'pupil involvement and ownership', 'widening notions of achievement in all learning contexts', 'positive portrayal', 'description rather than grades', 'grounding assessment in evidence' and so on.

Records of achievement have three crucial functions in relation to the assessment issues discussed in this chapter. First, they hold the potential to bring into a single coherent framework the various elements of formative assessment discussed earlier. In this sense RoAs may serve as a conceptual and practical 'umbrella' which infuse the processes of formative assessment with a broader rationale. Second, as a set of philosophical principles they may serve as a 'foundation' upon which the kinds of changes to teaching styles, classroom management and the organisation of learning described above may be carried out. Finally, records of achievement enable teachers to report the narrow and possibly insubstantial progress, which pupils make in relation to national curriculum attainment targets, to be reported in the broader context of their personal and social achievement. Records of achievement have broken significant new ground in describing individual pupils' learning in terms of general skills, processes and competences.

This approach to reporting is perhaps especially important for pupils with special educational needs, at a time when government policy appears to be placing undue emphasis upon narrow conceptions of learning within a subject-based curriculum. Most expert commentators in the area of special needs, including the Fish Report (ILEA, 1985), have drawn attention to the need for building assessment procedures upon a definition of progression in learning informed by an identification of the skills, processes and competences at the heart of educational aims and objectives, rather than conventional academic subject structures. As I have argued above, this principle is relevant to *all* pupils, but possibly particularly so for pupils with special needs. There can be no denying that the National Curriculum, and its attendant assessment arrangements, are constructed upon an entirely different set of principles. There can, moreover, be no denying that the government's lamentable decision *not* to establish a national framework for records of achievement (DES, 1989b) has been widely understood as a setback for the cause of 'records of achievement for all'. Nevertheless, records of achievement represent the only approach which can preserve the traditions of child-centred, process-orientated teaching and assessment in the area of special

141

education. Most local education authorities, to their credit, have committed themselves, as a matter of policy, to substantial support for the development of RoAs — not only for SEN pupils, but for pupils of all abilities and aptitudes. There is therefore considerable ground for optimism that, as we move into a new and uncertain era of educational change, teachers of pupils with special needs may receive the support necessary to *record* pupils' successes and not merely to *report* their failures.

References

Barrs, M, Ellis, S. Hester, H. and Thomas, A. (1990) *Patterns of learning: The primary language record and the national curriculum,* London: Centre for Language in Primary Education.

Broadfoot, P. James, M. McMeeking, S Nuttal, D. and Stierer, B. (1988) *Records of achievement: Report of the national evaluation of pilot schemes,* London: HMSO.

Broadfoot, P. Grant, M. James, M. Nuttall, D. and Stierer, B. (1991) *Report of the national evaluation of the records of achievement pilot scheme extension,* London: HMSO.

Department of Education and Science (1988a) *National curriculum: Task Group on Assessment and Testing: A report,* London: DES.

Department of Education and Science (1988b) 'Kenneth Baker sets out principles for assessment and testing in schools' (DES News 175/88, 7 June 1988).

Department of Education and Science *English for ages 5 to 16,* London: DES.

Department of Education and Science (1989b) 'Reporting pupil achievement under the national curriculum', (DES News 265/89, 16 August 1989).

Gipps, C. Gross, H. and Goldstein, H. (1987) *Warnock's eighteen percent: Children with special needs in primary schools,* Lewes: Falmer Press.

Inner London Education Authority (1985) *Equal opportunities for all?* (The Fish Report), London: ILEA.

Russell, P. (1990) 'The Education Reform Act — The implications for special educational needs', In: Flude, M. and Hammer, M. (Eds.) *The Education Reform Act 1988: Its origins and implications.* Lewes: Falmer Press.

School Examinations and Assessment Council (1989) 'Assessment of Pupils with special educational needs', quoted from the *SEAC Recorder* No.2 in National Curriculum Council, *Curriculum Guidance 2: A Curriculum for all: Special educational needs and the national curriculum,* York: NCC.

Tunstall, P. (1990) 'Review article: 'A guide to teachers assessment, Packs, A, B and C' (SEAC)' in *Curriculum* Vol.1 No.2.

Wedell, K. Evans, J. Goacher, B. and Welton, J. (1987) 'The 1981 Education Act: Policy and provision for special educational needs', *Special Education*, Vol.14, No.2, pp.50-3.

Wragg, T. (1990) 'Who put the ass in assessment?' in *The Times Educational Supplement*, 16 February 1990.

(Editorial Note: The speed of change and development regarding assessment and recording procedures by the Government is such that the account provided in this chapter can only relate to circumstances at the time this book went to press. Nevertheless, the issues discussed have a continuing and current vitality.)

The Editors

Neville Jones is a Regional Tutor in Special Educational Needs at the Open University. He was Principal Educational Psychologist with the Oxfordshire County Council Education Department from 1976 to 1990. During this period he directed the Oxfordshire Disaffected Pupil Programme and was the editor of a new series of books on *Education and Alienation,* published by Falmer Press. He has edited *School Management and Pupil Behaviour* (1989), and three volumes of *Special Educational Needs* (1989-91). He has co-edited *Teacher Training and Special Educational Needs* (with J. Sayer, 1985); *Management and the Psychology of Schooling* (with J. Sayer, 1988); *The Management of Special Needs in the Ordinary School* (with T. Southgate, 1989); *Refocusing Educational Psychology* (with N. Frederickson, 1990); *Learning to Behave* (with E.B. Jones, 1992); and *Education for Citizenship* (with E.B. Jones, 1992).

Jim Docking was formerly Chairman of the School of Education and Head of Education at Whitelands College. Before entering higher education he taught in schools in Yorkshire and Coventry. He now works freelance, running courses for serving teachers.

Dr Docking's PhD thesis was on the development of children's attitudes towards personal responsibility. He is editor of *Education and Alienatation in the Junior School,* and author of *Control and Discipline in Schools: Perspectives and Approaches,* now in its second edition (1987), *Primary Schools and Parents: Rights Responsibilities and Relationships* (1990), and *Managing Behaviour in the Primary Schools* (1990).

Contibutors

Mel Lloyd-Smith is Lecturer in Education at Warwick University.

Margaret Peter is Editor of the *British Journal of Special Education.*

Jennifer Evans was formerly a Senior Research Officer at London University and is a Specialist Assistant on Special Education to the House of Commons Select Committee on Education.

Ingrid Lunt is Senior Lecturer in the Department of Educational Psychology at the Institute of Education, London University.

Deborah King is a parent governor, having trained as a teacher at Moray House College, Edinburgh.

Hilary Shuard is Director of the PrIME Project at Homerton College, Cambridge University.

Peter Knight is Lecturer in Education at the University of Lancaster.

Alan Farmer is Principal Lecturer and Head of History at St. Martin's College, Lancaster.

Nigel Proctor is Senior Lecturer in Geographical Education at Manchester Polytechnic.

Mary Greaves was formerly Principal Careers Officer with the Oxfordshire County Council.

Dorothy Sydenham is an Adviser with the Oxfordshire County Council Education Department.

Barry Stierer is a Staff Tutor with the Open University.

Index